Come, Have Breakfast

Come, Have Breakfast

Meditations on God and the Earth

Elizabeth A. Johnson, CSJ

Maryknoll, New York 10545

Third Printing, December 2024

Founded in 1970, Orbis Books endeavors to publish works that enlighten the mind, nourish the spirit, and challenge the conscience. The publishing arm of the Maryknoll Fathers and Brothers, Orbis seeks to explore the global dimensions of the Christian faith and mission, to invite dialogue with diverse cultures and religious traditions, and to serve the cause of reconciliation and peace. The books published reflect the views of their authors and do not represent the official position of the Maryknoll Society. To learn more about Maryknoll and Orbis Books, please visit our website at www.orbisbooks.com

---

Published by Orbis Books, Box 302, Maryknoll, NY 10545-0302.

Manufactured in the United States of America

Library of Congress Cataloging-in-Publication Data

Names: Johnson, Elizabeth A., 1941– author.
Title: Come, have breakfast : meditations on God and the Earth / Elizabeth A. Johnson, CSJ.
Description: Maryknoll, NY : Orbis Books, [2024] | Includes bibliographical references.
Identifiers: LCCN 2023033953 (print) | LCCN 2023033954 (ebook) | ISBN 9781626985643 (print) | ISBN 9798888660225 (ebook)
Subjects: LCSH: Creation—Meditations. | Nature—Religious aspects—Christianity.
Classification: LCC BT695.5 .J634 2024 (print) | LCC BT695.5 (ebook) DDC 261.8/8—dc23/eng/20231116
LC record available at https://lccn.loc.gov/2023033953
LC ebook record available at https://lccn.loc.gov/2023033954

For people who band together at the international, national, and local levels to protect Earth's land, water, and air and all living beings; for government officials who do the same; for those who teach ecological care to children; for people who take individual action such as turning their lawns into habitats for pollinators.

In a particular way for the global Laudato Si' Movement galvanized by Pope Francis's letter of the same name, whose mission is "to inspire and mobilize the Catholic community to care for our common home and achieve climate and ecological justice, in collaboration with all people of good will."

Contents

Introduction

The great living God of heaven and Earth who made the sea and all that swim in the waters, the skies and their flying birds, the solid land and all the creatures that grow, slither, burrow, lumber, or walk upon it on two or four or more legs, this great Love brought forth the beauty and bounty of the evolving world out of sheer unfathomable goodness. At the same time, while determining the number of stars and calling each of them by name, this same ineffable Giver of life has the biblical reputation of being gracious and merciful, hearing the cries of the poor, loving justice, freeing the enslaved, healing the brokenhearted and binding up their wounds. Not only Creator, then, but also Redeemer, of human beings and of the whole creation. One ancient prayer recognizes it this way, "O God of our salvation, you are the hope of all the ends of the earth and of the far distant seas" (Ps 65:5). Another psalm affirms, "You save humans and animals alike, O good Lord" (Ps 36:6). In response to this infinite, empowering affection, creation praises the living God, Earth sings for joy or cries for help, the heavens tell of divine glory and, to those who ask, the beasts teach about the hand that made them.

Such is one way to describe the biblical picture of God and the Earth in relationship. In tune with this source, the meditations in this book try to decipher the heart of God toward creation in order to widen our own minds and hearts for ecological care.

A word about the title. "Come, have breakfast" are the words of the risen Jesus in the Gospel of John (21:12). It is an interesting project to ask people if they can identify who in the Bible said these words. The majority draw a blank. Compared with other sayings of Jesus, such as "Love one another," or "Blessed are the poor," or "This is my body," his invitation to breakfast is practically unknown. It appears in a story where Jesus feeds his disciples after they have been fishing all night. He has a fire going on the beach, with bread and fish cooking, and calls these tired men to partake of the meal he has prepared. In the story itself, the inviting words "Come, have breakfast" are obviously an expression of Jesus's care for the bodily well-being of the fishers. Reading this gospel in our time of ecological crisis, the invitation opens onto a wider perspective. "Come, have breakfast" is a bugle call of divine hospitality toward all people and all living creatures, revealing a passionate divine desire that all should be fed. Pulsing from the story is a call to the community of disciples of Jesus to act on behalf of nourishing others.

These meditations are written in face of the awful fact that our planet is in trouble. Earth is a beautiful place with a dazzling diversity of life, in fact the only place in the universe where life even exists, so far as we know to this date. But in our day it is undergoing strong physical changes that are damaging the very future of life.

Much good work is being done, from international legal agreements to individual life-style changes. Even with good will, however, the challenge is unprecedented. Think of it: dealing with the ecological crisis requires that people of many nations and vastly different cultures across the continents collaborate responsibly on a complex planet-wide problem with ramifications into the far future for generations yet unborn. The human race has never had to do this before. Making the effort harder, care for the Earth faces fierce opposition from ideological, political, corporate, and financial forces. And we cannot underplay indifference.

Meanwhile, the climate emergency continues to worsen, wreaking havoc on land, sea, and air with their plants and animals, while the resulting chaos disrupts the lives of ever more millions of human beings, increasing hunger and death and turning many into climate refugees.

Amid this complex scene, the ecological agenda has made its way into the world's religions as seen in the teaching of their leaders, the practice of many faith communities, and projects of interfaith cooperation. Since religious traditions at their best are bearers of wisdom about the ultimate meaning of it all and lay out a roadmap for how to live a good life, most have an inner dynamism that can nurture ecological engagement. Pope Francis put his finger on this resource when he wrote in the encyclical *Laudato Si'*:

> I would like from the outset to show how faith convictions can offer Christians, and some other believers as well, ample motivation to care for nature and for the most vulnerable of their brothers and sisters. . . . It is good for humanity and the world at large when we believers better recognize the ecological commitments which stem from our convictions. (*LS* 64)

In other words, beliefs have consequences. Belief in God can count for something in the practical order. It is here that these meditations linger, because I think the general idea of God needs a little work.

While never denying that God created the world and all its creatures, Western Christian teaching and practice for much of its history have focused mainly on human beings as beloved recipients of divine care. The rest of the community of creation has formed a backdrop to the drama of human salvation. Said to be created for human use, the natural world was not of direct interest either to God or to believers. Not only does this view shortchange the richness of biblical teaching about salvation, but the devastating climate emergency gripping our planet renders it woefully inadequate. Wrecked ecosystems and the extinction of thousands of plant and animal species along with misery for human communities, especially those most vulnerable and afflicted with poverty, cry out for a spiritual attitude more generous in its ecological commitments. An immense task facing theology in our day is to help turn the church toward beliefs and practices of faith that include the whole planet, indeed the whole cosmos, in what is religiously important.

In truth, Christian understanding about God's relationship to human beings is tremendously valuable and needs to be preserved. In the light of ecological destruction, it also needs to be expanded. It needs to bring forward the truth that the living God created an entire community of creation and is passionately in love with the whole shebang. It needs to help us appreciate that the heart of God surrounds even the tiniest creatures with affection. In this light we need to reimagine what it means for God's human creatures to be part of God's whole creation and act accordingly.

In addition to faith convictions, another source of motivation for care of the Earth was identified by the scientist Stephen Jay Gould. In his insightful words, "We cannot win this battle to save species and environments without forging an emotional bond between ourselves and nature as well—for we will not fight to save what we do not love." He was writing to support TV programs, books, and school lessons about nature, along with local parks, bird walks, anything that would increase people's visceral contact with the natural world. Being exposed to its beauty or learning even a little bit about how it works, he rightly argued, awakens wonder and leads to love with the desire to protect.

This motive can but deepen people's love for the Giver of life who quickens the world into being and compassionately sustains its dynamic evolution at every moment.

Hence these meditations. Each is a snapshot that presents but one aspect of the God-Earth relationship. There are dozens of different angles to the subject. I would suggest that you, good reader, might well benefit from pondering these short pieces one at a time rather than reading straight through from beginning to end. This would give you a chance to muse about each particular point, to see if you agree or disagree, to discover if it enriches your understanding, your prayer, your action. One or another may catch your attention in a special way. You may want to skip around, according to your interest.

Taken all together, these meditations present something of a panoramic view of the living God who loves planet Earth and accompanies all its inhabitants in their living and dying with the intent to save, having particular care for those who suffer from social and ecological injustice. The aim is to open up an angle of vision so that when anyone says the word "God," a picture of the changing Earth enfolded with divine affection reflexively comes into view, along with whatever else one is thinking, teaching, preaching, arguing, or praying about. No God without Earth! No Creator without creation! No Singer without her song!

These meditations focus specifically on the God-Earth relationship that is underdeveloped in the Christian imagination. But affection for the world around us does not present us with an either-or choice between commitment to the Earth or to other human beings. "We have only one heart," as Francis wrote (*LS* 92). The same cruelty that leads us to mistreat an animal will show itself in our relationships with people as well. By contrast, a deep sense of communion with Earth's living beings awakens concern for humans too, with special attention to the unjust inequality that mires people in desperate and degrading poverty or prejudice with no way out. Everything is connected. We are all woven together by the love of God and we stand or fall together.

Each meditation begins and ends with a scripture verse taken from the Bible, especially the psalms. Many of these are hidden gems, often overlooked. The German theologian Karl Rahner once wrote that some words are like seashells "in which can be heard the sound of the ocean of infinity, no matter how small they are in themselves." They are words that bring light to us, or evoke the blinding mystery of things; words that pour out of the heart and open the doors to great truths; words which by a kind of enchantment produce in the person who listens to them what they are expressing. The biblical words that form bookends to each meditation have something of this seashell quality. You may want to carry one or other away like a mantra.

It may be asked whether the subject of God is even relevant in the midst of ecological disaster. The various fields of ethics would seem more germane. Thankfully, excellent studies in ecological ethics abound. Some works uncover connections between unjust systems of human domination, such as racism or sexism, on the one hand, and disparagement of the Earth, on the other. Some analyze the ways in which economic systems create both ecological harm and entrenched human poverty in the drive for profit. Exploring the intersection of ethics and spirituality, yet other studies focus on the sin of human ruination of the Earth and develop dimensions of the virtue of earthkeeping. Still more present cogent moral principles that promote human responsibility for ecological care.

This book's meditations on God and the Earth support such valuable ethical probing, thinking, arguing and exhortation. They also focus on another vital dimension, the idea of God in relation to the Earth, which is basic to the whole discussion.

Why is this? Because the symbol of God functions. It lodges deep within the psyche and powerfully molds the identity and values of a faith community and its members, shaping their commitments, their actions, and their hopes. The large-scale change of human minds and hearts known as ecological conversion, so necessary in our day, requires in part a transformation of images deep within the psyche, and in particular images of the divine.

James Michener put this insight into bold relief in his historical novel *The Source*. As he tells it, there was an ancient Canaanite village where people worshiped various gods, including one who required human sacrifice. The lives of firstborn sons were especially precious; their sacrifice ensured ongoing fertility of crops. A young woman named Timna had recently given birth. In love with her newborn, she could not accept that he must die. Desperately she argued and pleaded with her husband, but her vigorous protests were of no avail. On a given day, amid great public ceremony, her husband walked to the altar and handed the infant over to the priests, who tumbled the little bundle into the flames. Months later, still consumed with grief, she attended another community ceremony. "And while others celebrated she walked slowly homeward, seeing life in a new and painful clarity: with different gods her husband Urbaal would have been a different man."

With different gods her husband would be a different man. The spiritual wisdom in this fictional woman's insight is profound.

Imagine a continuous, public understanding of the living God as passionate Lover and Savior of the Earth and all its creatures, including human beings, in the community of life. Imagine we understood that we are part of something bigger than our basically good, sometimes dreadful, always fascinating selves, something that has value of its own in God's eyes. Imagine our hearts growing to include the whole community of creation in our love of neighbor, so that action on behalf of social justice and ecojustice flow organically rather than being add ons to faithful living. Imagine churches praying, preaching, teaching, repenting, lamenting, praising, and acting so as to do justice to the heart of the living God who pours out love on all human beings as well as on the soil, the waters, the air, and every little bird that falls to the ground, as Jesus taught.

With a different God, the people of God would be a different people.

These meditations hope to contribute toward this kind of faith-filled ecological sensibility, to practical and critical effect.

Elizabeth A. Johnson, CSJ
New York City
July 22, 2023, Feast of Mary Magdalene, Apostle

Creation: A Relationship

1

Your creatures

O God, how manifold are your works!
In wisdom you have made them all;
The earth is full of your creatures.
—Psalm 104:24

The wild animals of the forest are mine,
and the cattle on a thousand hills.
—Psalm 50:10

Pronouns matter

The personal pronouns in these prayers call for attention. "Your creatures," referring to God, and wild and domestic animals that are "mine," also referring to God: what is the meaning of this language? Does anyone look upon a cow grazing on a hill and think it belongs to God? Probably not. Still, these pronouns, which show up throughout scripture, give voice to a deep religious intuition, namely, that these are creatures of a generous, loving Creator who gives them life.

Even at their most ferocious and magnificent, all creatures of earth, including humans, come into being and pass away. The powerful process of evolution can explain how they took shape over the course of time, and why they die. But in an ultimate sense, the fact that they exist at all does not explain itself. The vulnerability of their lives gives rise to a sense that their being here at all rests on a foundation other than themselves. This is where the idea of creation comes in. As biblical faith sees it, their existence is due to the creative action of God, whose generous goodness brings them into being and whose loving power continuously supports their vitality. In turn, they are ultimately reliant on the presence of God in every instant for their life, given and received as a gift. Hence, the diverse creatures are "yours," the wild animals are "mine." There is a personal relationship at the heart of it all.

Continuous creation

Ordinarily the mention of God creating the world takes our minds back to the origin of things. The dramatic opening words of the Bible tend to keep our gaze on the past: "In the beginning God created the heavens and the earth . . ." (Gen 1:1). While never explicitly saying so, people often assume that after this initial spark of God's creative activity everything rolled along on its own. It is almost as though the Creator's rest on the seventh day extended into a long retirement.

What gets overlooked in this shortsighted view is the truth that the act of creation is ongoing. The living God continuously creates. Without this largess, there would be no world at all. With it, Earth with its endless varieties of amazing creatures embedded in diverse ecosystems continues to evolve. The personal pronouns "yours" and "mine" convey the spiritual sense that the dynamic presence of the Creator undergirds, enfolds, and bears up the natural world, its processes and its creatures, at every moment.

A beautiful metaphor dreamed up by a British philosopher expresses the kind of active relationship at play. The Creator "makes all things and keeps them in existence from moment to moment, not like a sculptor who makes a statue and leaves it alone, but like a singer who keeps her song in existence at all times." Creation as a live musical performance! While the musician keeps singing, the music lasts. When she stops, the show is over.

The music of creating entails that an unbroken outpouring of divine goodness upholds the existence of the world in every instant, while creatures exist with an absolute reliance on this life-giving power for their own existence and action. Divine creativity is active here, now, in the next minute, or there would be nothing at all. Theology traditionally speaks about this music in the language of Spirit. Difficult to pin down in one image or idea, the Creator Spirit is the dynamic personal presence and activity of the living God who is profoundly near while remaining a holy mystery of love beyond what we can understand or imagine.

The relationship forged by the act of creation is the framework in which the intimate belonging of "yours" and "mine" finds a home. Let us ponder this ongoing creative relation of God to the world and the world to God in the midst of time, which itself is one of God's creatures.

Creator empowering creatures

The question of why there is anything at all, why there is something and not nothing, finds an answer in the basic character of the Creator: "God is love" (1 John 4:8). The living God is love, faithful, challenging, and compassionate love as the scriptures often declare, self-communicating love as recent theology makes bold to say. This love is the wellspring of creation. There is no pressure on infinite holy mystery to create and continuously support a world. How could there be? It is done freely, as a flaming, generous act of love, the plenitude of infinite love overflowing. With simple reasoning one biblical book figures it this way: "For you love all things that exist, and detest none of the things that you have made, for you would not have formed anything if you had hated it" (Wis 11:24).

The living God's way of creating is *sui generis*, genuinely one of a kind. When humans create, whether it be a baby, a book, a building, a business, a law, a theory, a garden, a website, a recipe, a protest sign, a song, it is always done with material at hand. By contrast, the often-used traditional Latin phrase *ex nihilo*, "out of nothing," points to the unfathomable act of God's originating all things and continuously keeping them in existence with no material at hand, no intermediary, no pressure, no pre-existing conditions.

Poetic images abound. God speaks and the power of that word brings the world into being: Let there be, and lo! there it is. Again, God molds a human figure out of the dust of the earth and breathes the spirit of life into its nostrils, and it becomes a living being. Both are images in the book of Genesis. Like a woman giving birth, like a potter casting clay on a wheel, like a bird brooding eggs into hatching, like an artist making a beautiful work of art, God makes a world. These and other biblical images hint bravely at how we might imagine the relationship of creation. None, of course, can be taken literally. But each one keeps front and center the connection between Maker and what is made.

Creatures participating in the Creator's liveliness

The cattle on a thousand hills and all other creatures receive the liveliness of being by participating in the gift of existence according to their own different natures. The Creator gives with great affection; creatures receive. Nothing in the great world would exist but for this constant relationship. Rocks, plants, animals, human beings, ecosystems, stars, galaxies, universes—without the ongoing creative power of God at every moment, all would collapse into the abyss of "nothing," an unimaginable no-thing. Owing one's existence to the ongoing creative love of the living God is the core meaning of being created. As the apostle Paul so beautifully riffed on some Greek poets, God is not far from any of us, for it is within this life-bestowing presence that "we live and move and have our being" (Acts 17:28).

No relationship could be closer.

Ponder the sense of all things existing and interacting dynamically within the relationship of creation, with the Creator Spirit present everywhere, vivifying every creature, sustaining every speck of matter and energy in the world. There is so much to appreciate.

> *The wild animals of the forest are mine,*
> *and the cattle on a thousand hills.*
> *I know all the birds of the air,*
> *and all that moves in the field is mine.*
>
> —Psalm 50:10–11

2
Kin in the community of creation

When you send forth your spirit they are created,
and you renew the face of the earth.
—Psalm 104:30

Kinship of the circle

As it has taken shape in life on Earth, the gift of creation has resulted in millions of species of astonishing variety, including the human species, *Homo sapiens.* Together all form a planetary community of beings who emerged from powerful natural processes. When seen through the lens of creation faith, all of these millions of different creatures have a radical relationship with their Creator. All share the identity of being cherished by God, whose very essence is love. All are born and die enfolded within divine affection. In the interim their every breath is sustained by God's creative Spirit. All species are included in this great picture.

Herein lies a challenge. The human species is marked by strong and unique abilities. We have the capacity for symbolic thinking along with the ability to express thoughts in verbal language. The result has been intense development of cultures. Unlike other species, we have spread across the globe, inhabiting almost every ecological habitat from cold to hot, wet to dry, north-east-south-west. We tell stories. We ask questions. We dream dreams about the future. We make ethical choices, good and bad. We invent and test things. We do business. We explore nature as well as our own bodies and spirit. We discover the age of the universe. We wreck the atmosphere. We comfort and heal. We rape and kill. We have the capacity for the most profound self-giving love as well as the capacity for self-delusion and for acts of barbaric evil.

Given these abilities, it has become common in religious and secular traditions of the modern era to think of human beings as standing apart from the natural world, with its multitudes of living beings, rather than being an interwoven part of it. Take, for example, a common interpretation of the opening chapter of the Bible. The first chapter of Genesis shows God creating the whole world and all its creatures on land, sea, and air. It ends with God giving the male and female human beings, who are made on the same sixth day as other land animals, a vocational call to have dominion over the fish, birds, and other living beings. In its original context, this divine commission gives humans a special responsibility to take good care of all the rest. Over time and especially in the modern era, however, the meaning of dominion has shifted to mean domination. Humans have the right to command and control. Even when the theme of stewardship is introduced to obligate human consciences to act responsibly toward the natural world, the story is read as favoring human separation from and superiority over the rest.

For a species such as we are, praying the great creation prayer Psalm 104 is an eye-opener. In stanzas of lyric poetry this prayer presents the whole world as God's good creation, as does the Genesis story. But instead of painting a hierarchical picture of creation with humans created last and exercising authority, this psalm depicts human beings embedded as fellow creatures in a community of creation. Humans show up in the middle of the psalm amid a loose arrangement of plants and animals in various landscapes, all related as kin benefitting from the Creator's largesse. Here the structure of creation is more like a circle with humans in the mix, not a pyramid with humans at the pinnacle. Let us ponder this sensibility so as to grow in a fundamental sense of kinship.

Beauty in every direction

Psalm 104 begins with enthusiastic praise for God's greatness in creating major landscapes. Stretching out the sky like a tent, God makes the clouds and takes joy in the weather: "you ride on the wings of the wind." The dry land gets put on a firm footing: "You set the earth on its foundations." The deep seas cover the land like a garment, but, remembering the great flood, "You set a boundary that they may not pass."

With the main habitats in place, living creatures make their appearance. First up are wild animals drinking and birds twittering and cheeping, all thriving with access to abundant water:

> You make springs gush forth in the valleys;
> they flow between the hills,
> giving drink to every wild animal;
> the wild asses quench their thirst.
> By the streams the birds of the air have their habitation;
> they sing among the branches.

Next come domestic animals and people, both being nourished by the fruitfulness of the land:

> You make grass grow for the cattle,
> and plants for people to cultivate,
> to bring forth food from the earth:

wine to gladden the human heart,
    oil to make the face shine
    and bread to strengthen the human heart.

What wonderful Mediterranean plants! Grapevines, olive trees, and stalks of wheat are gifts from the earth that give humans joy, beauty, and strength. Along with their domesticated cattle grazing on grass from the fertile land, these people present a picture of flourishing. Beyond human settlements great trees like the cedars of Lebanon are soaring:

In them the birds build their nests;
    the stork has its home in the fir trees.

In addition to shelter for animals who tend to stay local, God makes habitats for animals who need room to roam:

The high mountains are for the wild goats;
    the rocks are a refuge for the badgers.

People and animals live by a daily rhythm. They come and go, work, eat, and sleep on regular schedules. The Creator provides for these life-giving cycles by creating day and night:

You have made the moon to mark the seasons;
    the sun knows its time for setting.
You make darkness, and it is night,
    when all the animals of the forest come creeping out.
The young lions roar for their prey,
    seeking their food from God.
When the sun rises, they withdraw
    and lie down in their dens.
People go out to their work
    and to their labor until the evening.

Sun up, out come the humans. Sun down, out come the lions and other wild animals. At this point, overcome with the wonder of all this dynamic life, the psalm interrupts its description of the world to salute the Creator:

> O God how manifold are your works!
> In wisdom you have made them all;
> the earth is full of your creatures!

Birds singing in the branches, wild animals drinking from the streams, cattle chewing grass, lions hunting, people drinking wine and going to work; all these living beings are "your creatures." There is yet more, given the immense waters that border the land:

> There is the sea, great and wide;
> creeping things innumerable are there,
> living things both small and great.
> There go the ships
> and Leviathan that you formed to sport in it.

It would seem that the psalmist is something of a landlubber. Unlike fine-tuned descriptions of animals of land and sky, there are no particulars given for any sea creature. However, the writer does know that the waters hold a vast population of living things of all sizes, swimming and crawling, too many types to count. At least we can see the sailing ships plying their trade routes; they too belong to the sea. This mention of an artifact crafted by human skill once again paints human beings into the greater, wider picture of creation. Leviathan, a great sea monster, is another story. In most ancient texts this is a mythical giant sea serpent symbolizing chaos; it must be defeated for orderly life to continue. Here, rather than being a danger, the giant beast is created by God to play in the waters. Might it be the great whale, breaching, crashing back into the sea?

Gathering up the creatures from land, sky, and sea, the psalm points to their Creator as the ultimate source of all that nourishes them:

> These all look to you
> to give them their food in due season;
> when you give to them, they gather it up;
> when you open your hand, they are filled with good things.

Grass, worms, insects, bread and wine, little prey mammals, smaller fish, whatever living beings need to stay alive and thrive, these creatures too come from the generous hand of God.

Life is not all growth and development, however. Everything that lives eventually dies. This same Creator who makes and feeds creatures and arranges suitable habitats is intimately involved in their death:

> When you hide your face, they are dismayed;
> when you take away their breath, they die
> and return to their dust.
> When you send forth your spirit, they are created,
> and you renew the face of the earth.

Knowing that the word for spirit in Hebrew (*ruah*) also means wind and also means breath, we get a sense of how closely the breath of creatures and the spirit of God are interrelated. The life and death of all creatures is in God's hands while the work of creation goes on.

This magnificent psalm ends on three quick notes. First and very endearingly, the psalmist hopes the Creator finds joy in this amazing world vibrant with life: may you rejoice in your works! Next, the prayer's composer certainly appreciates it and its splendid Maker: "I will sing praise to my God while I live!" Lastly, rounding out the picture of a beautiful creation with the reality of sin, the one who prays hopes that wickedness will vanish and not deface God's work on the earth. Alleluia!!!

A CLOSER LOOK

What an array of divine activities seldom connected with God this psalm presents! Giving drink to wild animals; causing grass to grow for cattle; bringing forth grapes, olives, and wheat for human beings; watering trees; making a home for storks; feeding lions and other wild predators; filling the sea with animals from small minnows to great sharks: the verbs sound a steady drumbeat of divine attention to all creatures. Walking meditatively through this psalm awakens a view of creation as one connected community of different beings. Note that humans are not created last as a kind of apex of achievement as in Genesis 1. Nor do humans receive any call to have dominion over the rest. Rather, they belong intertwined with the creative bounty, dynamism, suffering, and death of other living beings in the natural world. Along with the cattle munching on the grass, people eat good things from the earth, although, unique among the species, they have to craft their wine, oil, and bread from cultivated crops. Along with the innumerable beings of the sea, they move around in their ships through the water. The breath of life in them, as with others, is a gift. When the breath leaves them, they die and return to their dust. They are renewed by the breath or spirit of God. While the psalm does not ignore the skills and ingenuity of people, these are set within the skein of life shared with others, not above or outside of the community of creation.

This psalm makes it stunningly clear that to believe in God the Creator is to appreciate the worth of other creatures and to know our kinship with them, all of us being created and forming one beloved community. In view of the distinct abilities we human beings possess and self-consciously *know* we possess, it is vitally important to dwell on this interconnected picture. Before emphasizing differences, let our thinking start with this profound unity. At the deepest religious root, precisely as creatures of the one God, *we humans have more in common with other species than what separates us.* In the telling words of *Laudato Si'*, "we are not disconnected from the rest of creatures but joined in a splendid universal communion" (*LS* 220).

In no way does this deny human distinctiveness, which is part of the glory and misery of the world. In no way does this lessen human responsibility to care for the earth, our common home, and to love it as God does. In fact, being part of the community means that the special capacity of human beings entails a special obligation toward the rest. Still, the deep theological truth marking human identity to begin with is that we are kin with all others in God's beloved creation.

It is one of the blessings of our era that scientific study reaches a similar conclusion by its own distinctive methods. In a cosmic framework, *Homo sapiens* is an intrinsic part of the evolutionary network of life on planet Earth, which in turn is a part of the solar system, which itself formed out of the dust and gas of older exploding stars in the Milky Way galaxy. Biologically, all living species evolved from common ancestors in the ancient seas and share a genetic history. Chemically, we are all of a piece with the universe. Why is our blood and the blood of other animals red? Because of hemoglobin which contains iron and, as one scientist observed,

> Every atom of iron in our blood would not have been there had it not been produced in some galactic explosion

> billions of years ago and eventually condensed to form the iron in the crust of the earth from which we have emerged.

The landscape of our imagination expands when we realize that our connection to nature is so deep that we can no longer truly define our human identity without including the great sweep of cosmic history and our shared biological inheritance with other organisms in the evolutionary history of life. According to science as well as theology, there is but one community of life on Earth. In scientific terms, there is one biosphere. In theological terms there is one community of creation. The natural world on Earth is a living whole. Everything is connected to everything else, and we all flourish or wither together.

To know God as Creator is to appreciate that all creatures, including our human selves, are beloved and related as kin in one community of creation. Let us ponder this community until we can no longer say the word God without seeing planet Earth and all its inhabitants as part of whatever story we are telling.

> *When I bring clouds over the earth and the rainbow is seen in the clouds, I will remember my covenant that is between me and you and every living creature of all flesh.*
>
> —Genesis 9:13–15

3

Go, have an adventure!

Thus says God, the bountiful Lord,
who created the heavens and stretched them out,
who spread out the earth and what comes from it,
who gives breath to its people
and spirit to those who walk on it:
I the faithful Lord have called you for justice.

—Isaiah 42:5–6

Making

Ancient biblical writers, imbued with faith in God's creative power, described poetically how God stretched out the heavens, laid firm the foundations of the land, gave the sea instructions to stay within its bounds. Their model of the cosmos put an unchanging Earth at the center with the sun, moon, and other heavenly bodies circling around it under the dome of the sky, which is actually the way things appear to the unaided human eye.

Many centuries later we have a different understanding. Scientific discoveries have led us to see the heavens and the earth as the still-unfinished result of natural processes. Five or so billion years ago on an outer arm of the Milky Way galaxy, our sun was formed from the dust and gas expelled by a previous generation of exploding stars. Gravity pulled the swirling debris together, shaping it into a new star with its orbiting planets, Earth being the third one out. Evidence suggests that early in our planet's history a large object crashed into it, gouging out the moon. The science of plate tectonics traces how continents have formed and moved about; when the India landmass rammed into the Eurasian plate, the pressure thrust up the immense Himalaya mountain range, which is still growing taller. Ice ages with their moving glaciers carved out river valleys and land formations, such as the Hudson River and its palisades. Volcanoes keep on bringing up molten rock from the planet's fiery interior. In our day sea levels are rising, inundating coasts and drowning ocean islands. The air itself is growing warmer; instead of being expelled, the sun's heat is being trapped in a blanket of gases rapidly accumulating from humans burning fossil fuels. Since life began on this planet more than 3.5 billion years ago, different species of plants and animals have evolved in sync with this changing environment, emerging and disappearing. All these points are subjects of investigation and debate, at times leading to reliable consensus about how things came to be.

Not a static planet, then, but one in constant flux. The ingenuity of human creatures in figuring out how the planet works is itself a marvel.

The Bible with its belief in a Creator who makes heaven and earth and all that is in them was written centuries before this modern knowledge developed and should not be expected to possess it. What remains constant for faith, whatever model one uses to envision Earth, is the religious intuition that the living God has an ongoing creative relationship with land, sea, air, and their inhabitants that enables their existence and actions.

But how should we understand the belief that God makes the world at the same time that cosmic forces make and biological evolution makes? The ambling character of life's evolutionary emergence over billions of years, which entails genuinely chancy occurrences and the enormity of suffering and extinction, is hard to reconcile with a simplistic idea of God the Creator at work. Let us ponder the meaning of creation with this question in view.

To what will you compare me?

The problem is unsolvable if one envisions God as a particular being among other beings, like a human person who acts, only with more power and might. The problem gets worse if one envisions God along the lines of an all-powerful monarch ruling his realm, as has traditionally been the case. The king—for God is traditionally envisioned as a powerful male person—designs the way things should run and lays down laws that must be obeyed. Creatures act in the way the ruler intends. Everything is planned out in detail. Under the sway of this image, God is thought to act directly as a factor within the network of the world's natural causes, making planets, creating foxes, whipping up hurricanes, deciding that this human baby rather than that one should be born with a genetic defect. "He" slips in as a kind of powerful force of nature, a cause among other causes. In this view, the integrity of the natural world that develops by its own natural processes is compromised, if not suffocated altogether.

Best to let go of the idea of God as a monarch acting upon other beings. Move your mind in the direction of the living God who is infinite holy mystery. Sit with the truth that our finite minds cannot comprehend the One who is infinite; our finite hearts cannot grasp love without limit. Look toward God not as an individual actor within the range of creatures but as the unimaginable personal Source of all beings, the very Ground of being, the Beyond in our midst, a generative ocean of love,

Creator Spirit. Then begin to realize that the power of the Creator Spirit is not exercised as raw power over but as love that empowers-with. God's creative activity brings into being a universe endowed with the innate capacity to evolve by the operation of its own natural powers, making it a free partner in its own creation.

Expanding our view of the living God along the lines of the paradigm of the lover opens a way to respect the genuine autonomy of nature's operation and the freedom of creatures' behavior that the Creator God makes possible.

The paradigm of the lover

The literature on love could fill whole libraries. Consider one form of love that can serve as a worthy though imperfect analogy for God the Creator. Among human persons a mature loving relationship builds up the strength of personal autonomy in those loved, whether they be on an equal footing like spouses or friends or at different stages of life like parents and children, teachers and students. Rather than suppressing the gifts of the other, love brings about their flourishing. Rather than stifling the power to act freely, love promotes its growth.

Not all manner of relationships do this. In controlling, manipulative, fearful, narcissistic, and egocentric relations, one party seeks to gain advantage by bending the other to his or her own will. The core integrity of the other is disrespected by ploys meant to dominate. Mature love operates with the opposite dynamic. Parents rejoice when their child walks, talks, shows interest in the world, grows into a functioning, contributing person. Teachers rejoice when their students learn skills, pose questions, and begin to think for themselves. Friends, including those partnered in marriage, rejoice when the beloved grows in ability, confidence, power to be uniquely themselves. In our fractured world love is never perfect, always mixed with other forces. On balance, however, its effect is life-giving; its energy brings about profound growth toward genuine autonomy.

In similar yet always dissimilar fashion, it is typical of holy mystery who is Love, mature divine love, to create a world endowed with the innate capacity to develop in its own way by natural processes. Such self-giving love creates, blesses, and enhances creatures' inborn capacity to act inventively. With such a love there can be no anxiety about control.

Have an adventure

As God's good creation, the world becomes a free partner in its own becoming while the Creator enables its existence at every moment. To put this succinctly, God creates the world by empowering the world to make itself. Far from compelling the world to develop according to a pre-designed plan, the Spirit continually calls it forth to a fresh and unexpected future.

Be imaginative for a moment. It is as if the Creator gave the world a push saying, "Go, have an adventure, see what you can become. And I will be with you every step of the way." In more classical language, the Giver of life not only creates and conserves all things, holding them in existence over the abyss of nothingness, but is also the dynamic ground of their becoming, calling from the future, empowering from within their emergence into new complex forms, like the cattle on a thousand hills and the birds singing among the branches.

It is interesting to discover how a hint of this sensibility is woven into the grand creation narrative of Genesis 1, though certainly not for scientific reasons. Notice the dynamic:

> Then God said: Let the earth bring forth vegetation, every kind of plant that bears seed and every kind of fruit tree on earth that bears fruit with its seed in it. And so it

> happened. The earth brought forth vegetation, every kind of plant that bears seed and every kind of fruit tree that bears fruit with its seed in it. And God saw that it was good. (Gen 1:11–12)

Even in this religious myth of origin, no contradiction exists between recognizing God as Creator of all things and seeing that the Creator invests the earth with the active power to bring forth plant life. The same dynamic continues with the seas: "And God said, Let the waters bring forth swarms of living creatures" (Gen 1:20). In this instance, the text switches back to divine action bringing forth sharks and crabs: "So God created the great sea monsters and every living creature that moves, of every kind, with which the waters swarm" (Gen 1:21).

Biblical creation texts express the belief that the world subsists on a foundation other than itself, thanks to which it is vital and generative. Clearly, the view that the world is God's good creation is a religious affirmation, one not afforded by the workings of natural science. It is the expression of a basic trust that the world has a radically transcendent origin, support, and goal, a view that gives the world a profound meaning. At the same time, this belief does not negate the way the world develops according to natural laws. The dynamic presence and activity of the Creator Spirit undergirds and bears up the integrity of all evolutionary process.

God and the world do not compete. The earth and the waters bring forth life with innate creaturely power because the fecundity of the land and sea is itself a divine gift.

Utmost generosity

The living God acts by the divine power of love in and through the autonomous operation of the world, which acts according to its own dynamic laws. This is not to say that God's action mixes with creation's action, which has its own wholeness. On the contrary, the great-hearted God "makes" by imparting to creatures the dignity of making things happen. Hills rise, streams gush forth, wild asses drink, trees grow branches, birds nest in them and sing, all thanks to the free operation of natural geological and evolutionary causes. This includes chance occurrences and random mutations that open up the status quo, ignite what is unexpected, and make new things freshly possible. Faith sees the awesome Spirit of God empowering it all.

Let us ponder the vis-à-vis of creation until it becomes impossible to say the word "God" without honoring how the bounteous God loves the world into being as a free partner in its own making.

All the ends of the earth have seen
the salvation by our God.
Sing joyfully to the humble Lord, all you lands;
Break into song; sing praise.

—Psalm 98:3–4

4
A suffering world

You, O God, are gracious and merciful, slow to anger and abounding in kindness.
You are good to all, and compassionate toward all you have made.

—Psalm 145:8–9

The cost of evolution

For all its extraordinary beauty, Earth is a planet of pain. Meditating on creation, we cannot ignore the overwhelming magnitude of suffering and death that marks the history and experience of life. Mention of suffering usually brings to mind the experience of human beings. As embodied creatures we are subject in natural ways to physical and mental illness; we suffer emotionally from life's setbacks, loneliness, and loss; inevitably we grow old; we die. In addition, there is the unnatural brutal harm people inflict on each other by war and violence, by systemic racism, poverty, discrimination on the basis of gender and sexual orientation, and by meanness and cruelty of all kinds. The terrible litany goes on and on.

Other conscious beings in the world also suffer.

Consider what happens every day. In every ecosystem predators hunt and devour their prey; prey animals grunt, sigh, or shriek in their death throes; eventually even predators die. In a new form of affliction, human beings engage in factory farming. We raise large numbers of animals in tight, unnatural quarters that subject them to a miserable existence before they are slaughtered for food. In our day, too, humans are encroaching on natural habitats to such an extent that thousands of species are rapidly going extinct. Animal studies show that consciousness is experienced on a spectrum. What humans experience as physical pain as well as the emotional pain of fear, terror at threats to one's own life, and grief over loss of another is experienced in various ways by other animals according to their own natures. All suffer.

On a wider scale over deep time, life itself evolves at a terrible cost. Evolution requires generations. Small mutations in egg, sperm, or embryo may result in progeny better adapted to a change in the environment. The new descendants outpace the elders, eventually emerging into new species. The old disappear. Death is deeply structured into the creative advance of life, which arises in the midst of perpetual perishing.

Herein lies a paradox. Clearly there is horrific suffering. At the same time in and through this affliction, "endless forms most beautiful" in Darwin's lovely phrase, keep on emerging, propelled by the inner evolutionary dynamism of life itself. As one memorable example highlights, "the cougar's fang has carved the limbs of the fleet-footed deer, and vice-versa." Through their interaction over generations, the cat's teeth get sharper, the deer runs faster. Taking the long view, we can see that without struggle and death there would be no emergence of new creatures, no wings, eyes, or brains: no soaring creatures in the sky, no fine-tuned eyesight registering color and shape, no advanced crafty minds. Without pain, no further exploration of life's potential forms; without death, no new life. These afflictions arose as essential elements in the powerful process of evolution that created and continues to create the magnificent community of life on this planet.

However marvelous the results, the suffering is staggering. It runs like a red thread through the history of life. If we ask "Where is God in the midst of this misery?" and hear the biblical answer "Here," in solidarity with creatures crushed by pain and finished by death, a stunned silence ensues. What kind of a Creator God is this?

An unfinished world

One rationale in the current literature holds that, since the evolving world is not yet finished, we should not be surprised that situations turn out to be messy and painful. Suffering and dissolution abound because the world is still under way. We should not expect everything to be perfect. There is profound wisdom in this insight into creation as incomplete and still on the move. Nevertheless, such an assessment is no comfort to broken bodies and distraught feelings, to ruined communities and wiped-out cultures, to wasted habitats and extinct species.

Others speculate that while God does not directly will the world's suffering and death, divine wisdom allows it for some higher purpose. In the case of humans this might be to punish sin, or to teach patience and other virtues, or to enable people to merit a heavenly reward. Trying to justify God in this way, a project known as theodicy, has a long and vigorous history. But for the most part today, these traditional answers have lost their traction. They no longer work in the face of what we know about the cost of evolution, to say nothing of mass murder, genocide, and other horrors inflicted by human hate. Critics point out that, by trying to rationalize agony as somehow rooted in God's "plan," theodicy itself becomes an evil. It ignores the voices of victims. It cuts the nerve of resistance to injustice, because if this be the divine will, then we should suffer rather than resist. It also ignores the pain of sentient animals who are not human. It seems to make God into a monster who allows grievous suffering while remaining unaffected in distant heavenly glory. Overall, the intellectual effort of theodicy fails because it tries to set up a logical explanation for what is beyond reason.

My own sense is that suffering and death are too much of an enigma to submit to such logic. Rather than theodicy, what is needed is reflection that takes suffering as a given and ponders the reality of God in its terrible light. More needs to be brought into view about the Creator who knows what creatures are suffering and is with them through thick and thin with the promise of something more. More needs to be said about the living God who is merciful and compassionate, identified in the flesh of Jesus with the crucified and the dead. More needs to be understood about the Spirit of love profoundly present amid breakdown to inspire breakthroughs. With a fuller understanding of God we can grasp that the Creator is in alliance with the suffering world, a source of hope.

The burning bush

The conviction that the Creator of heaven and earth is with creatures in times of trouble, opening up hope for their future, is bedrock to biblical faith. In my view one of the most moving, brilliant scenes where this truth shines through is the burning bush event in the biblical book of Exodus. At first glance it might seem that by dwelling on a story focused on the liberation of an enslaved people we have wandered far from the subject of creation. But to the contrary, there is only one God, who is not compartmentalized. The Creator is also the Redeemer. The One who makes the world out of love is also the One who saves the world because of that same love. Scripture puts it this way: "You are good to all, and compassionate toward all you have made" (Ps 145:9). A close reading of the dialogue at the bush on fire but not consumed brings to light in narrative form a radical insight into the compassionate presence of God across the whole created world.

As the story opens, the Hebrew people are being oppressed as slaves in Egypt. Setting in motion a process to free them, the word of God comes to a man in the wilderness; he is in exile for killing an overseer who was beating a slave. God calls to him, "Moses, Moses!," and he responds, "Here I am." Hearing that it is the God of his ancestors Abraham, Isaac, and Jacob who is speaking, he takes off his sandals; this is holy ground. Then come words of incredible compassion:

> I have seen the misery of my people who are in Egypt; I have heard their cry because of their taskmasters. I know well what they are suffering; therefore I have come to deliver them. . . . Now go, I am sending you to Pharaoh to bring my people, the Israelites, out of Egypt.
> (Exod 3:7–8, 10)

Notice the "I." In four stunning verbs the Creator of the wild, good world *self-identifies* as the holy God who sees the affliction of enslaved people, who hears their groans, who feels their misery, and who acts to liberate them. The third verb takes on greater resonance when we realize that the word "know" used here is the same Hebrew word used to describe sexual intercourse in Genesis: "Adam knew his wife and she bore a son" (Gen 4:25). Obviously, "I know well what they are suffering" connotes an intimate, experiential kind of knowing. Not far away or distant, oblivious to trouble, God is in feeling solidarity with their wretched trouble.

Let it not escape notice that God started the process of liberation by inspiring a man with a checkered background into action: "Go, I am sending you." At this point Moses was tempted to back away from his originally generous response, "Here I am." Living life on the margins of Pharaoh's kingdom, he was a most unlikely candidate for this dicey task. Who am I, he protested, to do such a thing? In later texts he will say he stutters or has some kind of speech impediment; send someone else. God responds with a simple but utterly profound promise: "I will be with you." If nothing more were said, this pledge alone would reveal that the One who comes to liberate will keep faith with this man, will not abandon him.

But there is more.

Still reluctant, Moses says that if he goes to the people and says the God of their ancestors sent him, and they ask for this God's actual name, what should he tell them?

> Then "God said to Moses, 'I am who I am.' . . . Thus you shall say to the Israelites, 'I am has sent me to you.'" (Exod 3:14)

Here we are at the heart of a revelation of mystery. The original Hebrew of this name has no direct equivalent in translation. It can be anglicized in the letters YHWH, which are printed as Yahweh. The name is not gendered. Out of deep reverence, Jewish tradition became unwilling to pronounce it. The usual English translation is "I am," or "I am who I am." Later thinkers in Greek culture took this in a philosophical sense to mean God's nature is being, source of the being of all creatures. The ancient Hebrews, however, thought more in terms of God's operation and attitude toward them rather than of God's essence. Jesuit theologian John Courtney Murray suggested that, as originally heard, the divine name had a relational, intersubjective meaning. Catching this cadence, a more adequate rendering of the mysterious name YHWH would be "I shall be there as who I am will I be there with you." Awe-inspiring mystery of absence (as who I am), God becomes God-with-the-people (I shall be there).

The story unrolls. Moses goes. The God of the mysterious name is with him. The future opens up for an enslaved people, although not without the messiness of history.

God of a Suffering World

This is a very particular story of a people's enslavement and their move toward freedom. But the exchange at the burning bush sears into consciousness a truth that is always and everywhere the case. The Creator Spirit is present amidst suffering with the intent to heal, redeem, and liberate. Write this truth large across the struggles of all human beings. And because God is faithful to all of beloved creation, write it large across the community of life on Earth. In creating the world God is present here and now to each creature, loving it into existence and promising its future. When trouble comes, the Creator does not turn tail and flee. Ever faithful, the living God does not abandon the beloved creature but is present despite the suffering, in fact in the midst of it. As Australian theologian Denis Edwards mused in eloquent language:

> The Creator Spirit is with creatures in their finitude, death and incompletion, holding each in redemptive love, and is in some way already drawing each into an unforeseeable eschatological future. This promise points to a participation of all creatures in the dynamism of di-

vine life. The Spirit is with each creature now, with every wild predator and prey and with every dying creature, as midwife to the unimaginable birth in which all things will be made new.

Things fall apart. There is hope for the future. "I will be with you" is the proper name of the Creator of heaven and earth.

I shall be there, as who I am will I be there with you.
—Exodus 3:14

5
Here we are!

The stars shone in their watches and were glad;
God called them, and they said, "Here we are!"
They shone with gladness for the One who made them.
—Baruch 3:34–35

Baruch's scenario of the star-maker God calling to the stars and their glad response expresses the ongoing relationship of creation in a poetic vignette. The Creator Spirit continuously gifts each being with the flame of its own existing and accompanies it into the future, while each thing shines with the gift according to its own nature. A loving relationship is at the heart of it all. To see the natural world respond to its Maker in the language of "Here we are" is to express this core relationship poetically. It doesn't mean we think the stars are actually conscious. Their very existence is a song of sorts.

It is easy to overlook this. For one thing, contemporary Western culture does not automatically defer to the existence of God, and this affects our attitude like the air we breathe. The world is just there; it is what it is. For another thing, attention among Christians usually focuses more intensely on Jesus Christ and the grace of human salvation, with little spillover to the natural world. In our time, however, faith in God brings the natural world to the fore as the recipient of an infinite Creator's merciful care.

"Here we are!" Only three little words, but they hold a powerful sense of mutual presence, calling and responding, Creator to creature and creature to Creator. Let us ponder the relationship of creation through the lens of this saying.

Human response

The author of the book of Baruch obviously drew on the experience of human creatures responding joyfully to God when he imagined the stars shining with gladness. Our human response may indeed be glad, but it may also be confused, vastly reluctant, or even set in opposition. Many people do not have a conscious experience of responding to the living God at all. The Jewish writer of this book drew on his own faith tradition about creation and saw that a particular human religious experience had parallels among the shining stars.

Throughout the scriptures "Here I am" is a recurring response, almost like a mantra, which people give when they sense God's approach calling them to an important task that will affect the future. Abraham and other ancestors of the Jewish people used this response: "The angel of the Lord called to him from heaven and said, "Abraham, Abraham!" And he said, "Here I am" (Gen 22:11). At root the words bespeak a relationship of trust on the part of the human creature. Here I am, standing by, on high alert, listening and discerning, sleeves rolled up, maybe not too sure but ready to do what seems right, ready to do your will, responding to your call, let's go. The readiness is rooted in a hopeful conviction that the living God is present and active with gracious intent and will be with the person wherever the road ahead leads.

In Abraham's case, the first call was to leave his country and go "to the land that I will show you," accompanied by a promise that in him all the families of the earth would be blessed. Centuries later a New Testament writer had a great insight about this moment: "and he set out, not knowing where he was going" (Heb 11:8). Such an honest comment. As always, the future was unknown, even scary. But by taking the first steps with trust that God would be faithful, Abraham with his wife Sarah and her servant Hagar started a segment of history down a new and blessed path.

"Here I am." Moses said these words in response to the voice from the burning bush sending him to free an oppressed people (Exod 3:4).

"Here I am." Three times in one night the young Samuel woke up his mentor with these words, until Eli perceived that it was God who was doing the calling and directed the lad to respond, "Speak, Lord, for your servant is listening," finally allowing his old self to get back to a good night's sleep (1 Sam 3:9).

"Here I am." With these same three words prophets like Isaiah indicated their willingness to serve: "Here I am; send me" (Isa 6:8).

"Here I am." A village girl of Nazareth, poor but highly favored, spoke them as she set out on the adventure of bringing the Savior into the world: "Then Mary said, 'Here I am, the servant of the Lord; let it be with me according to your word.' And the angel departed from her" (Luke 1:38).

"Here I am." In a terrifying scene anticipating the horror that lay ahead, her son Jesus spoke the equivalent: "Father, if you are willing, remove this cup from me, yet not my will but yours be done" (Luke 22:42).

Through the ages people who answer to the promptings of the Spirit and follow their conscience, no matter how hard the doing or the letting go, are kin to their ancestors in the faith as well as to the stars in their reply. Here I am. Here we are.

Grasping the deep mutuality at play, the prophet Isaiah channeled God's gracious response with the same words:

> Then you shall call, and the courteous Lord will answer;
> you shall cry for help, and God will say, "Here I am."
> (Isa 58:9)

Not all human beings respond to the promptings of their conscience or to the call of the Spirit with a generous "Here I am." The human response is complex and never coerced. The call to act justly, love tenderly, and walk humbly with your God may be accepted but it may also be refused. Ravaging harm is done by humans to other people and to the earth in acts that religious language calls sin. Even here the call of the living God does not quit. The gift is not like the transgression. "Where sin abounded, grace abounded all the more," declared the apostle Paul in view of Christ crucified and risen (Rom 5:20). In a more contemporary vein the theologian Karl Barth put it this way: "God says 'Yes'; we say 'No'; God says 'Nevertheless.'" The tough loving-kindness and faithfulness of the Creator is without end, ceaselessly calling, comforting, and challenging humans onto the right path, opening up the future.

Creation's response

With a parallel kind of freedom, the expanding universe as a whole evolves according to its own natural processes. Galaxies, stars, planets, asteroids come into being and pass away. Things merge into new forms and crash and die in ways that are not totally predictable. Belief in God who creates and redeems the world trusts that powerful divine love sustains the whole enormous process through all the beauty and disasters, calling it into a future promised but unknown. That same creation faith can see the world's ongoing emergence as a kind of creaturely response: "Here we are."

In our own corner of the universe, our beautiful blue marble of a planet that carries the freight of biological life is also enfolded in this creative relationship. Earth is full of God's "loving-kindness," God's "steadfast love," God's "mercy," God's "merciful love," God's "faithful love," God's "kindness," or God's "goodness" (Ps 33:5). In a kind of happy confusion, translators of this psalm cannot seem to land on a single word for the Hebrew noun *hesed*. Let us embrace all of the above. Their swirl ushers our minds and hearts toward a love beyond all telling.

One occasion that brings forth Earth's joyful response into view is a bountiful harvest. Throughout human history this has always been a cause for gratitude, ensuring as it does a sufficient supply of food for people and their domestic animals; they will not starve. Like Baruch's image of stars shining with gladness, the fertile earth too can respond with gusto:

> You visit the earth and water it, making it abundantly
> fertile.
> Your streams are full of water; you provide the people
> with grain...
> the hills are robed with joy;
> the pastures are clothed with flocks;
> the valleys blanketed with grain;
> they shout and sing together for joy.
> (Ps 65:9–14)

More than just beautiful nature writing, this prayer gives a grateful nod to the Source of all this fruitfulness, "You." With a bountiful harvest rolling in, the hills, the pastures, the fertile valleys are shouting for joy: Here we are! Human thanksgiving is implicit. Simply recounting the details is prayer enough.

All is not always beautiful and fruitful. In an uncanny parallel to our own time, scripture is replete with scenes of devastation caused by human wrongdoing. Vegetation withers, springs of water disappear, animal life deteriorates, fruitful land becomes waste and void, because human beings flout the moral order. The prophet Hosea described one such situation in dire terms:

> There is no faithfulness or loyalty, and no knowledge of
> God in the land.
> Swearing, lying, and murder, and stealing, and adultery
> break out;
> bloodshed follows bloodshed.
> Therefore the land mourns, and all who live in it languish;
> together with the wild animals and the birds of the
> air, even the fish of the sea are perishing.
> (Hos 4:1–3)

Now creation's glad response changes pitch and becomes a wail of sorrow. The vineyard is ruined, "desolate, it mourns to me" (Jer 12:11). "The wild animals cry to you because the streams of water are dried up, and fire has devoured the pastures of the wilderness" (Joel 1:20).

Does the relationship with creation perdure amid devastation? The creative presence of God, easier to experience amid beauty and bounty, seems absent from a world that is desolate. But the Creator of heaven and earth abides even amid destruction. Otherwise there would be no world at all. More than simply being present, biblical prophets insist, the God of creation sorrows for the world that is ravaged. Due to invasion sheer destruction reigns; God says, "I drench you with my tears" (Isa 16:9). In compassion and vulnerable love divine holy mystery takes up the cry of lament for people who are broken and land that is devastated. The enduring presence of God—"I will be with you"—

ensures that the suffering world continues, takes the next step, and does so with potential for healing, restoration, even the emergence of something new.

In our day

Far from affecting one country, one patch of land or one water system, global warming today is changing the weather pattern of the whole planet. Human beings will not stop burning fossil fuels. As a result, previously unthinkable extremes of drought and flood, wildfire and melting glaciers, rising sea levels and changing weather patterns are plaguing humans and all other creatures. The creation relationship is not destroyed in the face of this ruination. The Creator holds on. But now the joyful "Here we are" is turning into mournful cries, "Here we are, suffering and dying and going extinct." It is obvious what the faith response of "Here I am" is calling us humans to do.

There is only one living God, gracious and merciful, who creates and redeems the world and calls it into the future. Present and active always and everywhere, the Creator Spirit accompanies all creatures through the course of their time. Life on Earth, embedded in the universe as a whole, continues to evolve in greatness and beauty, not without terrible destruction, suffering and death, toward final union with the Omega. This is the fundamental dynamic of creation in dramatic terms:

Go. Here I am. Here we are. I will be with you.

When I called, you answered me,
you built up strength within me.
—Psalm 138:3

6
Creation's praise

Praise God from the highest heavens, sun and moon,
all you shining stars!
Praise God from the earth, you great sea creatures and
all ocean depths,
lightning and hail, snow and frost, stormy winds,
you mountains and all hills, fruit trees and all
cedars,
wild animals and all cattle, creeping things and
flying birds,
kings of the earth and all peoples, young men and
women alike, old and young together!

—Psalm 148, condensed

MAKE A JOYFUL NOISE

Look at the variety of creatures called upon to praise their Creator in this psalm. Creatures in the sky, on the earth, and in the sea! Brilliant stars! Elements of weather! Land formations! Vegetation! Animals of all kinds—wild, domestic, walking, creeping, flying! Human beings of all types! The whole community of creation is urged to form a chorus praising the Giver of life.

Found especially in the psalms, this theme of creation praising God runs through many biblical writings. While scripture texts using the exact word "praise" are relatively few in number, all kinds of creatures are called upon to bless God, give thanks, sing, shout for joy, roar, tell, acclaim, declare, give honor, magnify, glorify, exult, clap, or make a joyful noise. The wealth of synonyms reflects the belief that such activity is practically a universal occurrence. This is borne out by the climactic last line in the book of Psalms: "O let everything that has breath praise God!" (Ps 150:6). In the vis-à-vis relationship of creation where the living God continuously sustains the beloved world, this is the creaturely response. Yay! Aren't you wonderful! Thank you!

It is no exaggeration to say that for long stretches in the West creation's praise of God received little or no attention. With few exceptions such as the Celtic and Franciscan traditions, Christian thought and prayer focused mainly on God's gracious deeds for human beings that deliver, forgive, help, and redeem them. Rather than be included as a vital part of the story, the natural world and its creatures functioned as a stage set for the main events. Creation dropped even further from view in the long tradition of spirituality which held that in order for a person to ascend to union with the all-holy God, Earth with its flesh, its bodily pleasures, its pressures, sufferings, and struggles had to be left behind. But this is woefully to shortchange creation.

Let us ponder creation's praise. This activity has gone on for billions of years, long before human beings ever evolved to appear on the scene and join the chorus in a specially explicit way. Paying attention can stretch our minds and hearts to appreciate the wider world's relationship to its good Creator who loves and sustains it. What does it mean, this praise of God from all of creation?

Multiple meanings

Over time scholars have proposed a range of possible meanings that are interesting to ponder. Each sheds a little light.

❧ Seeking to understand the historical world of the biblical writers, scholars point out that psalmists and prophets had a *polemical* intent when they called upon the sun, moon, and stars as well as the animals to praise God. In other ancient Near Eastern religions some of these glorious beings were held to be gods, such as the sun god Ra in Egypt or the sacred bull in Mesopotamia. But here in Israel's prayer, instead of being worshiped, these things are themselves creatures who praise the one God who created them all.

❧ Another line of interpretation holds that all creation's praise will happen at the end of time. In technical terms it is an *eschatological* event, an event of the final future. This position sees the whole created order as having been skewed by human sinfulness that leaves it groaning, far from God. On the last day violence will cease, justice will be established, and God will reign over a new heaven and a new earth. On that day all creatures of the world will be freed up to join in giving praise. The book of Revelation carries this profoundly hopeful vision:

> Then I heard every creature in heaven and on earth and under the earth and in the sea, and all that is in them, singing, "To the one seated on the throne and to the Lamb, be blessing and honor and glory and might, forever and ever!" (Rev 5:13)

Notice that every creature is singing. Relegating creation's praise to the future in this way at least gives it a place in the religious imagination. However, it says nothing about what such activity might mean in the present.

❧ A more commonly held view takes a *literary* approach and interprets creation's praise of God as a metaphor. A versatile figure of speech, metaphor juxtaposes two different objects that play off each other: you are my sunshine; war is hell; all the world's a stage; the Lord is my shepherd; a mighty fortress is our God. The interaction between the two opens up aspects in each that might otherwise remain hidden. We understand them differently, with more nuance.

To say that creation's praise of God is a metaphor uses an activity that people know about from their own experience to illuminate the world's more unknown relationship to God. While this can lead to appreciating that the world indeed has a relation to its Creator, metaphor by its very nature does not stake out a claim in a literal sense. You and the sunshine are two different things; a mighty fortress and our God are not identical. Using metaphor results in assuming that whatever creation does, it is not actually praising God.

❧ Yet another view places human beings at the center of the picture. In this *anthropocentric* approach, the beauty of the world or the intricate behavior of its inhabitants awakens our wonder, which leads us to glorify the Creator who made them. In this way creation praises God indirectly though the human mediator.

The fifth-century theologian and bishop Augustine provides a classic example. In a sermon on Psalm 148 he preached that animals and plants praise God by inspiring human beings to give praise. Warming to the subject, he extolled a flea. Imagine being in the fifth-century North African congregation that heard this sermon:

> Let me have your attention, please, beloved. Who was it who so arranged the bodily parts of a flea or a gnat, that they would enjoy coordination, life, and movement? Study any tiny creature, any one you choose. I want you simply to consider the disposition of its organs and the life that animates it: look how it avoids death, loves life, seeks pleasures, avoids painful conditions, deploys its various senses, and flourishes in the mode proper to itself. Who gave the flea a stinger with which to suck blood? How tiny is the pipe through which it drinks! Who arranged matters so? Who made these things?

After more such marvelous description, Augustine concludes the sermon:

> But anyone who has eyes will study many of this world's creatures, and in studying them will find delight in them. When these things delight us we praise them, but not for themselves. We praise God who made them, and thus all creatures praise God.

The well-made flea, then, becomes an occasion for human prayer. But it does not praise in its own right. Humans become the sole conduit for animals' praise of God. Advocates of this view are wont to say that humans are the priests of creation, mediating between the world and its Creator, or that we are the cantors of the universe, singing praise in the name of all the rest. While indeed reflecting the human experience of praising God in face of nature's wonders, this position does not take the next step and do justice to the reality that all creation praises God in its own right. In view of the recent emergence of the human species on Earth, to say nothing of the historical time-span of the universe, it also leaves billions of years silent of any praise at all.

Robust creation theology

A strong creation theology offers yet another interpretation based on relationship. This does much better justice to God as Creator. The ever-loving God is continuously present to all creatures, empowering their existence. Each receives life, catching fire from the Source of all flame. Each is beloved, having intrinsic value in God's eyes. Together all form one community of creation. In this framework, creation's praise of God does not need human beings. Such praise is neither a projection of human consciousness onto other creatures nor a beautiful fiction, but a real action that occurs in real time. In their very existence, just by being there, in the way they interact in an evolving universe, in their concrete quiddity (to use a great medieval phrase), creatures pay tribute to the excellence of their Maker. Augustine, taking a different tack from his sermon on the flea, saw this when he wrote:

> Let your mind roam through the whole creation. Everywhere the created world will cry out to you: "God made me." . . . Go round the heavens again and back to the earth, leave out nothing. On all sides everything cries out to you of its Author; nay, the very forms of created things are as it were the voices with which they praise their Creator.

Their very forms are the means by which they give praise! This is the sacramental imagination at work, rooted in a deep creation theology. A tree does not need to be conscious of anything or do any special act in order to praise God. Simply by being and growing, offering shade, shelter, food and medicine, and serving as a nourishing nurse log for others when it dies, it gives praise to God. Falcons praise God by their swift flying, mating and kak-kak-kaking. Both tree and falcon give witness by their very existence to the creative power that is the infinite Giver of life. The same holds true for all creatures, including those in a predator-prey relation, for suffering and death do not separate creatures from the love of God. The world's praise is not an extra, added on to what it is, but the shining of its being, the overflowing significance it has in pointing to its Creator simply by being and acting as itself. This might be called a *relational* interpretation rooted in creation, in the gift of being.

With and without words

To say creation praises God is a faith statement. It is an interpretation shaped by belief in the ineffable holy mystery who creates and continuously empowers the world with loving-kindness beyond imagining. The idea does not add to scientific knowledge about the world nor does it change cosmic or biological discoveries in any way. Rather, the claim respects such data while placing all creatures in active reference to their ultimate origin, support, and goal.

In the human community, praise arises as a response to the great, life-giving presence of God and what God has done, this Holy One who made everything and is wonderful and redeems all. Most often praise is uttered in words, but it can also be expressed wordlessly in instrumental music or dance or body posture. At times it will pass over beyond words into silence, the silence itself being a salute to the incomprehensible Giver of life who cannot be captured in pictures or words. Whether verbal or non-verbal, human praise of God expresses a personal orientation of trust and gratitude. It answers back to the one who gives life.

As is the case among humans, the conscious language of articulate words is not essential for creation's praise. Recall the paradox posed by the beauty of the skies. The heavens are telling the glory of God, sings Psalm 19. Day by day they pour forth speech; night by night they declare knowledge. But how can this be? The heavens do not speak:

> There is no speech, nor are there words;
> their voice is not heard;
> yet their voice goes out throughout all the earth,
> and their words to the end of the world. (Ps 19:3–4)

There is more than one way to communicate. Anyone who has experienced the wonder of a starry night sky or a quiet rosy dawn, a clear blue day with the sun pouring down or an awesome approaching thunderhead has heard the soundless voice and wordless words of the heavens glorifying God.

We join our voices

Without hearing the voices of other creatures lifted in praise, our human minds and hearts could well overlook the real orientation to God embodied within the natural world. With this hearing, however, the world begins to witness for us a most profound truth. All of us together, humankind and otherkind alike, are fellow creatures of the same life-giving Creator. Together, we are all members of the community of life on Earth, engaged in complex interactions, sharing the world as a gift and task.

Midway through the third Eucharistic Prayer of the Catholic liturgy, the presider declares, "all creation rightly gives you praise." This is a fine thing to say at the heart of the Mass. Regrettably, the thought whizzes by as the prayer swiftly moves to call upon the Holy Spirit to bless the gifts of bread and wine and then repeats the words of Jesus on the night he was betrayed.

What an expansive sense of the loving Creator would result if at the start of every gathering for Christian prayer or liturgy the people called upon the ongoing praise of all creation which we humans now join. How magnificent to realize that the living God to whom we pray is also receiving the praise of the squirrel, the eagle, the trout, the firefly, the cactus, and the coral reef. We humans do not pray alone but form a chorus with a world of singers sharing the journey of life together. What desperately needed, responsible, self-sacrificing care of Earth and its species would flow as a result of such prayer.

The benefit can be mutual. At a time when prayer does not come easily to postmodern humans, becoming aware of nature's praise may actually allow these other creatures to help us pray. The more we attend to them, the more they can lift our hearts to God, borne on their praise.

O let everything that breathes praise God!
—Psalm 150:6

7
Animal praise to the God of all flesh

Praise God, all you wild animals and cattle,
you creatures that crawl and flying birds.
—Psalm 148:10

Scripture is threaded with verses that depict animals giving glory to God. At times individual animals are named, such as the wild jackals and ostriches in Isaiah's oracle: "The wild animals will honor me, the jackals and the ostriches" (Isa 43:20). In this case the animals are joining with the exiled Israelite people's praise for their Redeemer who is bringing them home. At other times animals are bundled together as part of their environment giving praise: "Let heaven and earth praise God, the seas and everything that moves in them" (Ps 69:34). Yet again animals are categorized by type: birds of the air, wild animals, domestic animals, creatures that creep and slither, as happens in the celebrative Psalm 148. The climactic prayer that closes the whole book of Psalms makes animal praise well-nigh universal: "O let everything that breathes praise God!" (Ps 150:6).

Musing on the meaning of honor given to God from the animal kingdom, it becomes clear that animal praise is nested within the religious framework of all creation's praise. It has the same basis, namely, relationship with the Creator, and the same meaning. As with the sun, the moon and the stars, the snow, the mountains and the fruit trees, so too with animals. In their own distinctive ways, by their very forms they give glory to God.

Animals pose a special case for our human understanding, however. Some species have a noticeable quality of awareness with intelligence, emotion, and ability to choose. How can we do justice to their praise without imagining them as little quasi-humans offering conscious, linguistic honor, thereby projecting our consciousness onto them? How can we humans even admit that God has a loving personal relation to animals without feeling threatened in our long-claimed superiority as a species? At the other extreme, how can we avoid the pitfall of dismissing animal praise of God as mere metaphor, delightful poetry without substance?

Let us ponder the truth that the Creator Spirit who is gracious and merciful has a direct relationship with animals. Scripture assumes this, given its sense of creation. The living God's loving relation to the fauna of our planet underpins the response of animal praise, imbuing it with a genuine integrity all its own.

A zoological gaze

On balance, the Bible is pervaded with what some scholars call a zoological gaze. This gaze sees a mutual relation existing between God and animals. It is a direct relation that does not require human mediation. Attending to some key texts has the potential to refresh our religious imagination on this point and lead us in an ecological direction.

From the divine side, so to speak, God creates animals, blesses them, and calls them good; makes a covenant with them; feeds and waters them; finds them suitable homes; delights in their ways; watches over them; cares about their deaths; saves them; and fills them with good things, foremost being the breath of life. The intimacy of this relationship comes to expression in biblical texts where God calls the animals "mine."

For their part, animals respond to this loving-kindness in their own unique ways by the working of their neurologically sensitive lives. They carry out the vocation to increase and multiply, thus participating in the ongoing work of creation; they cry to God for food and groan to God when it is lacking; they make intelligent use of their habitats; they teach and reveal divine truth to humans, when asked; and they praise divine goodness that is so concerned with their lives. Their orientation to God is captured in a telling image:

> The eyes of all look to you, and you give them their food
> in due season.
> You open your hand, and satisfy the desire of every living
> thing. (Ps 145:15–16)

Let us meditate on this relationship more closely.

❧ *Creation.* The foundational act is creation. Reading the creation story in Genesis 1 with the Creator's relationship to animals in mind, we find an intensity that may surprise. God creates swarms of creatures of every kind that move in the sea! Multitudes of winged birds of every kind that fly though the air! Living animals of every kind that dwell on land! The exuberant repetition of the phrase "of every kind" points to what we would call today the vast biodiversity of species that the Creator calls forth. Speaking directly to fishes and the birds, God blesses them and gives them the vocational charge to be fruitful and multiply. In other words, let's have more of your kind! On all the animals the unassailable judgment rings forth: "And God saw that it was good" (1:21, 25).

At the outset the hordes of creatures dwelling in sea, sky, and earth, the multitude of fish, winged birds, snakes, and wild and domestic mammals, along with plants and humans, all have their common origin in the overflowing generosity of the Creator who vivifies them and pronounces them very good.

❧ *Covenant.* The story of the great flood in Genesis ends by taking the Creator's relationship to animals to a new level. In a striking move, God freely initiates the special bond of a covenant not only with human beings but also with animals, both together. Before the flood, lest there be any doubt about leaving some animals behind, Noah hears the instruction to pay attention to every kind:

> And of every living thing of all flesh you shall bring two of every kind into the ark, to keep them alive with you; they shall be male and female. (Gen 6:19)

When the deluge recedes he hears a new pledge addressed to all the inhabitants of the ark:

> I am establishing my covenant with you and your descendants after you, and with every living creature that is with you, the birds, the domestic animals, and every animal of the earth with you. (Gen 9:9)

This covenant with Noah's family and with the animals is the first in the Bible's recounting. It precedes the covenants with Abraham, Moses, David, and the one established by Jesus. It is never revoked. The sign of this committed relationship will be the rainbow:

> When the bow is in the clouds, I will see it and remember the everlasting covenant between God and every living creature of all flesh that is on the earth. (Gen 9:16)

The designation "flesh" connects humans with animals in a materiality that is at once beautiful and vulnerable, filled with energy and subject to decay in time. Along with human beings, every animal of the earth, whether furred, feathered, or finned, "every living creature of all flesh that is on the earth" is in a vis-à-vis covenant relationship with the living God.

Such a bond means that animals are included in future blessing when God promises, "I will pour out my spirit on all flesh" (Joel 2:28). And it gives rise to a stunning divine title: "I am YHWH, the God of all flesh" (Jer 32:27). The creating, covenanting, living God self-defines as the God of the animals.

❧ *Sustenance.* Finding food and water as well as shelter to rear young is essential for species to survive. The One who creates and covenants is active on this front. One psalm takes note of how God "gives to the animals their food, and to the young ravens when they cry" (Ps 147:9). Conversely, animals know whom to ask: "The young lions roar for their prey, seeking their food from God" (Ps 104:21). As a member of the Jewish people, Jesus inherited this faith and expressed it in lyric tones: "Look at the birds of the air; they neither sow nor reap nor gather into barns, and yet your heavenly father feeds them" (Matt 6:26).

Abundance of fresh water, too, is a necessary, life-sustaining gift: "You make springs gush forth in the valleys, . . . giving drink to every wild animal; the wild asses quench their thirst" (Ps 104:10, 11). At the same time, animals know where to direct their groans when water is lacking: "the wild animals cry to you, because the watercourses are dried up" (Joel 1:20). In their distress they are counseled with words of comfort which elsewhere are directed toward anxious people: "Do not fear, you animals of the field," because God is restoring fertility with refreshing rain (Joel 2:22). Note that in these texts animal sounds, whether of young ravens, roaring lions, or suffering wild animals, are understood as cries to God.

In order to thrive, animals also need suitable habitats in which to dwell. The speeches from the whirlwind in Job 38–39 and the cascades of ecologically-attuned poetry of Psalm 104 depict the loveliness of diverse habitats the Creator provides for different species. Leafy trees for the songbirds, fir trees for storks, rocky crags for eagles, high mountains for wild goats and salt lands for swift asses—animals and habitats are all suited to each other.

Pursuing even these few biblical texts about the interactive exchanges between God and animals sets in high relief the realization that such relationality indeed exists and is mutual in both directions. The living God is deeply concerned for all the animals; they in turn respond in their own natural animal ways to the Creator's life-giving presence.

The ending of the book of the prophet Jonah carries the tenor of this relationship in a way that is almost humorous. The prophet is perversely peeved that the people of Nineveh have repented and will be spared destruction thanks to his preaching. Reprimanding him for his big sulk over this mercy as well as over the withering of a bush that had shaded him on a hot day, God asks:

> "Is it right for you to be angry about the bush?" And he said, "Yes, angry enough to die." Then the Lord said, "You are concerned about the bush, for which you did not labor and which you did not grow; it came into

> being in a night and perished in a night. And should I not be concerned about Nineveh, that great city, in which there are more than a hundred and twenty thousand persons who do not know their right hand from their left, and also many animals?" (Jonah 4:9–11)

Thousands of ignorant humans and also many animals: the Creator's merciful love encompasses them all.

Animal Praise

The relationship of divine creation, covenant, and sustaining care frames the context for understanding animal praise of God. Animals live in relation to their Creator. They go about their business as subjects of divine love. They respond by moving toward what is good and attractive in accord with their natures. They bear witness with their very existence to the creative power who is the Source of all. True, they do not articulate praise in human language. But as is the case even among humans, words are not of the essence.

An influential principle used by the thirteenth-century theologian Thomas Aquinas clarifies matters further. "Whatever is received, is received according to the mode of the recipient," he figured, or more colloquially, each creature receives and responds to the love of God according to its own nature. Thus, the way animals live precisely as animals articulates their praise. By virtue of their being created and continually empowered by the Creator Spirit, they praise simply by living according to their natures, which are oriented to God. Ken Stone eloquently summarizes the point:

> In the roar of lions, the flight of birds, and the surfacing and splashing of distant, mysterious sea creatures, the

> psalmists and other biblical writers heard or saw what they considered responses to a God who was believed to save—and also sometimes to judge— both human and animal. They heard and saw. . . animal veneration of God.

As part of the praise of all creation, animal praise refers not to a rhetorical device but to something that faith recognizes as taking place in the actual world. And it is a revelation. It discloses that animals are fellow creatures with their own relationship to God, responding with their lives to the Creator who has care for them.

In an age of ecological crisis marked by the extinction of thousands of species and by the struggle of millions of still-existing animals to find food, water, shelter, and migratory routes in the face of human encroachment, the reality of animals' praise of God shapes a faith that invites, persuades, even mandates human beings to act responsibly for the flourishing of our fellow creatures. Loving the God of all flesh motivates us to do nothing less.

Bless the good Lord,
you whales and all that swim in the waters;
sing praise and highly exalt God forever.
—Daniel 3:79

The Vivifying Presence of God

8
Earth, a dwelling place of God

Even the sparrow finds a home
and the swallow a nest for herself,
where she may lay her young,
at your altars, O vibrant protector,
my shepherd and my God.
—Psalm 84:3–4

The famous hazelnut

The infinitely loving Creator Spirit pervades the earth, its every nook and cranny, sustaining all living beings in their thriving, anguish, and death and empowering the whole world into its next moment. Such divine presence is encoded into the very core of what it means for the world to be created. The other side of this coin is that, rather than being distant from the divine, Earth is the dwelling place of God.

In one of her revelations about the courteous love of God, the fourteenth-century English mystic-theologian Julian of Norwich gave voice to this insight in her own ingenious way. She was contemplating Christ crucified, seeing his sacrifice as a sign of his love. Everything that is good and comforting for our help flows from this love. It is like a garment that wraps and enfolds us, embraces and shelters us, surrounds and never deserts us. Her vision of love's embrace then expanded beyond human beings to encompass all creation. She saw a little nut lying in her hand. Its round shape reminded her of the earth. Speaking to her understanding, Christ revealed its meaning:

> And in this he showed me something small, no bigger than a hazelnut, lying in the palm of my hand, as it seemed to me, and it was as round as a ball. I looked at it with the eye of my understanding and thought: What can this be? I was amazed that it could last, for I thought that because of its littleness it would suddenly have fallen into nothing. And I was answered in my understanding: It lasts and always will, because God loves it; and thus everything has being through the love of God.

Let us roll this hazelnut over in our minds, guided by Julian's insight. Starting with Earth, let our imagination extend to more distant and older swaths of the universe. Let us ponder how the same stunning truth holds fast at unlimited scale: "everything has being through the love of God."

The Presence of God

To be clear, speaking of God's presence in the natural world is faith language. We are not asserting such presence in a quantitative way as if this were one more ingredient added to physical processes, joined to material things, or inserted into biological life. This presence cannot be discovered by any scientific method or instrument, nor can it be included as part of any workable, practical theory. Instead, awareness of God's presence throughout the world arises first and foremost from a sense of wonder, that there is more here than meets the eye.

This sense goes way back in human experience. Almost all religions that human beings have developed regard the natural world as in some way a sacred place. Special trees, rivers, stones or mountain peaks, certain animals, particular moments in the sun's movement north or south, the fertility of the earth itself: on every continent stories and ceremonies give evidence that people have regarded the natural world as imbued with divine spirit, which gives rise to feelings of wonder, respect, and gratitude. In the monotheistic religions of Judaism, Christianity, and Islam, this sense is carried by the dear belief in a loving Creator who makes the world and dwells within it, empowering its life into the future.

In our day, popular culture as shown in cartoons and standup sketches reduces the ineffable mystery of God to an old, white, bearded man on a cloud saying stupid or funny things. Intellectual culture is rightly skeptical of such a supposedly Supreme Being. Even atheists who reject belief in God nevertheless assume that God is an elderly and male figure. Amid the swirling viewpoints it is easy to lose sight of the ever-present nearness of Creator Spirit.

But the living God is not an old white man—not old, not white, not a man at all. Clinging to this or any other image in a literal way leaves us with a puny godling. To create the entire world! To indwell the world! To accompany the world through dramatic changes! To promise the world a blessed future! To care for every individual human person and every creature who has ever lived, is living, or ever will live! To be present to billions and billions of moving galaxies! This requires an incomprehensible power of love so vast as to escape being captured by our minds. Certainly God is personal. But God is not a person in the limited way we experience ourselves and other human beings as persons. The living God is infinitely personal. God is personal as source of millions and billions of treasured persons, of all races and ethnicities and genders and sexual orientations and cultures. At this point we lose the finite concept of person to encounter what mystics call the bright darkness of ineffable holy mystery, who loves the little hazelnut.

A GRAIN

Just as the hazelnut inspired Julian's reflection on the creative presence of God, another little piece of earth, a grain, occasioned a meditation by Martin Luther, the sixteenth-century theologian and church reformer. How many grains of wheat are there? How many kernels of rice? Or of corn? How many seeds? Trying to answer puts us in the company of Abraham who was asked to count the grains of sand on the seashore or the number of stars in the sky. The answer is more than we can fathom. In that context, a grain of wheat is so minuscule as to be hardly noticeable. Envisioning a tiny grain against the scale of the whole universe, Luther mused:

> How can reason tolerate that the divine glory is so small that it can be substantially present in a grain, on a grain, over a grain, through a grain, within and without… entirely in each grain, no matter how numerous these grains may be? And how can reason tolerate that the same majesty is so large that neither this world nor a thousand worlds can encompass it and say, 'Behold, there it is'? Yet, though it can be encompassed nowhere and by no one, God's divine essence encompasses all things and dwells in all.

In, on, over, under, through, within, without—the piling up of prepositions focused on a small bit of plant matter sets up a shock in contrast to the magnificent array of multiple worlds imagined beyond it. But small or large, you can find the Creator Spirit in every grain and universe.

Presence

It would prove fruitful to play with Julian's or Luther's insight. Find a nut, a grain of rice or a kernel of corn. Place it in your hand and just sit with it for a time. While contemplating it with loving eyes, affirm the presence of the Spirit in, on, over, under, and through it. Slowly transfer your realization to everything.

The Spirit of God has filled the world.
—Wisdom 1:7

9
Like water, like air

Your imperishable spirit is in all things.
—Wisdom 12:1

Besides small bits of earth like a hazelnut or a grain, our planet offers other elements that may serve to awaken a sense of the Creator Spirit's life-sustaining presence beyond, with, and within all of creation.

WATER

Let your imagination play with water. In recent years a changing climate has produced fierce rainstorms and terribly destructive floods that prevent any innocent use of this symbol. Yet water is ubiquitous and essential for life. In salty form it covers three-quarters of Earth's surface. Coursing through the bloodstream, moistening every cell, water is found in every living creature. Deprived of it, they wither; supplied with it, they are refreshed. Is there water or ice on Mars? Then we might go live there.

The presence of the Spirit of God is something like water, often ignored but always at hand to invigorate. Augustine caught this in a lyrical meditation which we might join. First bring to mind the whole of creation, the land, sea, and sky, the stars, trees, and mortal creatures, everything seen and unseen. With this in our mind's eye, imagine it all floating in a sea:

> But Thee, O Lord, I imagined on every part environing and penetrating it, though in every way infinite: as if there were a sea, everywhere and on every side, through unmeasured space, one only boundless sea, and it contained within it some sponge, huge, but bounded; that sponge must needs, in all its parts, be filled with that immeasurable sea. So conceived I Thy creation, itself finite, yet full of Thee, the Infinite. . . .

Like a large sponge saturated through and through with ocean water, the world is dripping wet with divine presence. This does not forestall natural upheavals and changes, some beneficial and some disastrous, which are the way the world continues to take shape. Nor does it prevent agonizing suffering and death in sentient creatures, let alone every kind of human sin. What the presence of God holds out is mercy, ongoing energy for the next minute and hope for new life that will heal, redeem, and liberate, bringing refreshment to all.

Air

Let your imagination play with air and with wind, air in motion. At hurricane force or twisting in a tornado it can uproot, smash, blow apart, destroy livelihood and lives. Its power prevents any blithe use. Yet on a daily basis it is ubiquitous, intimate, an invisible presence necessary for the very life of all who breathe on the surface of the planet. Wind, breath, spirit, spirit of God: the Hebrew word *ruah* carries the connection between all of them. Something about air in motion points to the presence of God.

In the poet Gerard Manley Hopkins' description, air is wild, world-mothering, in and out of our lungs, nestled between every eyelash, flying through the spaces of the fleeciest snowflake, enfolding all. Capturing the mysterious quality of this element, Jesus put it this way: "The wind blows where it chooses, and you hear the sound of it, but you do not know where it comes from or where it goes. So it is with everyone who is born of the Spirit" (John 3:8).

Whether a gentle breeze or a mighty storm, the Creator Spirit like the air itself dwells everywhere in the world, blowing freely and affecting everything. Such presence cannot be corralled or enclosed, restricted or caged. Both in the natural and the human world, wherever this divine wind blows, something new is stirred up.

Love that moves

Divine *ruah* surrounding the little hazelnut, circling in and around a grain, saturating a sponge like a great sea, blowing though heaven and earth like the wind—in a time of ecological crisis such as ours, recovering awareness of the presence of God throughout the natural world comes as a challenging grace. Rather than being devoid of Spirit or even opposed to the divine, Earth is the dwelling place of God. Rather than a mere backdrop, it is the locus of divine activity deeply involved in, with, and under its open-ended evolutionary processes. The Creator loves the rich diversity of life on Earth, embedded in the tapestry of the cosmos, for its own sake and not only as a neutral stage on the way to the human species. To say this is not to detract from the singularity and importance of human beings, but it is to give value to the existence of the natural world as a subject of divine love. Dante once wrote eloquently of "the Love that moves the sun and the other stars." We can now riff that this Love also moves the Earth with its natural forces and living creatures, nearer to them than they are to themselves, acting always and everywhere within the matrix of the freely evolving community of life.

Encounter

Earth is a dwelling place of God, and thus it is a place where we can encounter God. In general, people's spirits pick up when they experience something of the wonder and beauty of the natural world. Getting outside is rejuvenating. Whether it be sere desert or green woods, grassy prairie or sandy beach, snowy mountains or fertile river valleys, a stand of tall trees or a single maple clothed in autumn colors, a city park or even a flower growing in an apartment window box, being in contact with the natural world has beneficial physical and mental effects. A belief in creation deepens these experiences. One can come across God in such places, sensing divine presence in the beauty.

All too often today some places in the natural world have the opposite effect. Poisoned by mining, burned by out-of-control fires, flooded, eroded, stripped, infested, polluted, dumped with garbage, they break one's heart and turn one's stomach. Such destruction led the biblical prophet Jeremiah to tell of divine tears over land that was devastated and animals that were decimated. He channels God saying:

> I will weep and wail for the mountains and take up a
> lament for the desert pastures.

They are desolate and untraveled, and the lowing of
cattle is not heard.
The birds have all fled and the animals are gone.
(Jer 9:10)

Even here, where life is throttled and choked, the Spirit of God is present with compassion, making a way out of no way.

As always, this takes the form of inspiring people to take action. The experience of the world being damaged often gives rise to the protest, "This should not be." The objection springs from an intuitive comparison between how we know the Earth should be and the devastation that threatens or now reigns. The negative contrast is based on a deep grasp of something good. The protest can lead to actions that resist, restore, and heal. Empathy itself becomes a powerful ecological force.

"*Earth's the right place for love:*
I don't know where it's likely to go better." (ROBERT FROST)

Appreciating the presence of God does not make the natural world all churchy. The oceans and clouds, the trees and the cats are just themselves, creatures, not explicitly spiritual things. They exist in their own natural ways, with their own integrity, and with a radical difference from God which is ultimately and essentially good. We encounter this goodness not by quickly looking past creatures to their Source, but by looking at them and appreciating their own quirky, irreplaceable quiddity, their simply being there with their multiple natural interactions. At the same time, faith sees that they exist because the loving Giver of life shares the plenitude of life as the grounding source of their existence at every moment.

Let us ponder the infinite holy mystery of God, not as a powerful individual at a distance, enthroned beyond hierarchical strata of greater and lesser creatures, but as Creator Spirit within and around the whole emerging, struggling, gorgeous, living, dying, evolving circle of life.

Where can I go from your spirit?
From your presence, where can I flee?
If I ascend to the heavens, you are there;
if I lie down in Sheol, you are there.
If I take the wings of dawn
and settle at the farthest limits of the sea,
Even there your hand shall lead me,
your right hand shall hold me fast.
—Psalm 139:7–10

10
Like fire that ignites

Shout joyfully to God, all the earth!
—Psalm 100:1

Fire is a major element on the planet classically used to symbolize the presence of God. In our day, the raging wildfires that destroy forests with their millions of wild inhabitants, ruin towns and human lives, and blanket cities with smoke prevent any simplistic use. Yet fire's beneficial properties of light and warmth, light to see by and warmth to comfort cold bodies and cook food, have long been used to symbolize the living God, infinite light and warmth.

In the twelfth century Hildegard of Bingen used the way fire spreads to illuminate divine creative action. Like the prophets of old she channeled the Creator Spirit, having God say:

> I, the highest and fiery power, have kindled every living spark. . . . I flame above the beauty of the fields; I shine in the waters; in the sun, the moon and the stars, I burn. And by means of the airy wind, I stir everything into

> quickness with a certain invisible life which sustains all. . . . I, the fiery power, lie hidden in these things and they blaze from me.

At the end of his popular book *A Brief History of Time*, which sets out the basic structure of the universe, physicist Stephen Hawking asks a famous question: "What is it that breathes fire into the equations and makes a universe for them to describe?" In the integrity of his adherence to atheism, he leaves the question open. Truthfully, there is no scientific answer to the question of why there is something rather than nothing. But this is not a scientific question. It is a question of wonder. And here faith offers a daring option, daring to believe that it is the Creator Spirit who breathes the fire of life into these equations, indeed, who fires up the equations to begin with. The Creator Spirit dwells within the world like a good warming fire. Wherever this divine fire glows, creation is sparked into luminous being.

God as a verb

Aquinas, too, used fire that ignites to illustrate the presence of God throughout the world. In his case, the symbol helps to visualize his more abstract but profound understanding of the creation relationship. Instead of thinking about the Creator as a particular person, as someone who speaks a word or crafts an item, Aquinas suggested we might think about the Love who created the world as a verb. The verb he uses is "to be," *esse* in Latin. Obviously this points to an action that cannot easily be put into images. It borders on a mystical understanding. The fundamental notion is that the Creator simply *is*, a sheer wellspring of existence. The verb form brings out the dynamic sense of be-ing.

The holy mystery of God is sheer exuberant aliveness, overflowing plenitude, the absolute act of existing without origin, without limitation, without end. In a word, the living God is the pure act of "to be." In creating the world God freely and lovingly gives a share in that aliveness, in being there, to others who are not divine. This creates a bond that cannot be broken. Trying to understand this, Aquinas wrote words that still resonate:

> God is in all things; not, indeed, as part of their essence, nor as an accident, but as an agent is present to that upon which it works.... Now since God by very essence is to be (*esse*), created being must be the proper divine effect, as to ignite is the proper effect of fire. Now God causes this effect in things not only when they first begin to be, but as long as they are preserved in being, as the sun causes light in the air as long as the air remains illuminated. Therefore as long as a thing has being, God must be present to it, according to its mode of being. But being is innermost in each thing and most fundamentally inherent in all things.... Hence it must be that God is in all things, and innermostly.

Innermostly! The way a flame sets other things on fire, the divine Source continuously sparks all things into being. The way the sun makes the air bright, the Creator shines the world and all its creatures into their own natural existence. Everywhere, from the minuscule to the magnificent, the Spirit of God quickens the creatures of the world at their core. At the same time, divine presence spills over beyond the interior of creatures, so to speak, and encompasses them on the outside as well. Hence, while "God is in all things," Aquinas observes, it is also the case that "all things are in God," inasmuch as they are "contained" or embraced by a living presence which cannot be limited in any way.

In ultimate terms every creature's existence with all its dimensions relies on the overflowing goodness of the Creator Spirit who freely shares "to be" with the world. The infinitely living God prodigally pours out existence on all things, sparking them into being, and finite creatures receive the spark and shine with creaturely flair. There is no individual, no place, no ecosystem, no process, no galaxy far far away, no thing and no time that exists or could exist without being empowered by divine love.

The omnipresence of God

It is unfortunate that teaching about creation has usually focused only on the origin of things. It is likewise a shame that when the term "supernatural" is used, it tends to confine the presence of God to places, times, and sacramental actions that are holy while everything else is simply "natural." This tends to lead to locating the experience of God on Sunday but not Monday, in church but not in the rest of the city or country. Frankly, such a divided world does not exist. The ongoing act of creation puts the living, all-holy God in direct relationship with the whole world and every one of its creatures at every moment or they wouldn't be there at all. The indispensable role of holy places, times, and sacramental actions is to make explicit and celebrate what is always and everywhere else the case.

Let us ponder the reality of the world sparked into being by the fire of divine love until it becomes impossible to say the word God without sensing the Spirit's presence throughout every inch of planet Earth. Together let us ask: why is this sense of divine presence in the community of creation not the default position of the praying church? Why is it so absent from everyday preaching and teaching, to say nothing of religious practice and public advocacy? We're missing something about God here.

> *The poor when they see it will be glad,*
> *and God-seeking hearts will revive;*
> *for the Lord of loving-kindness attends the needy,*
> *and does not spurn those in their chains.*
> *Let the heavens and the earth give praise to God,*
> *the seas and everything that moves in them.*
> —Psalm 69:32–34

11
The wisdom of the owl

Know that I the living God act with fidelity,
justice, and integrity on earth.
—Jeremiah 9:23

Imagine the possibilities

A favorite mind game of science educators invites us to turn the clock back to before the appearance of life on Earth, then hit the button and let the clock start ticking away again. Would the branching tree of life appear as it does now? Scientists are virtually unanimous in saying "no," so multiple and diverse, so genuinely open-ended and chancy are the factors that have come into play over billions of years to produce our planet's inhabitants.

Exhibit A would be the large asteroid that hit the Earth about 65 million years ago. The water vapor and rock dust it spewed up caused disastrous climate changes that resulted in the mass extinction of dinosaurs and more than half of the other fauna and flora on land and in the oceans. Afterwards, in emptied-out habitats, there was new room for some small surviving rodent-like mammals to evolve. Their branching lines eventually emerged into primates, hominids, and *Homo sapiens.*

Was that asteroid pre-programmed in some master plan to hit planet Earth, or did it do so by chance, following its own trajectory through space? The latter is the scientific answer. Amid the reliable operation of what we call the laws of nature, random events of great and small magnitude continually intrude, create havoc, break down the status quo, and open up the possibility for something new. The presence of chance operating within law-like processes means there is no guarantee at the outset of how life will turn out. In retrospect we can say that highly intelligent animal life might well develop, for the matter of the universe obviously has the potential to evolve into complex structures (brains) from which consciousness emerges. But without that asteroid, life on Earth would be a community with a different evolutionary history and hence with different kinds of species. Most likely we humans would not even exist.

This open-endedness raises in a specific way the question of what it means for God to create the world. It surely departs from the picture given by Genesis 1 where God's direct action makes different kinds of creatures and sets everything in its place. Not every person of faith wants to deal with this conundrum. But if your mind seeks a way of understanding, philosophy symbolized by the owl can shed some light. Aquinas's medieval discussion of causes proves to be a helpful tool.

The wisdom of causing

"As to ignite is the proper effect of fire," mused Aquinas, so too is creating the world the proper effect of the Creator. The infinite fire of being sets everything else on fire, so to speak. Let us follow Aquinas as he casts this image into the more abstract language of causing.

In general conversation, a cause is something that produces an effect; it makes something else happen. Faith in God holds that the ineffable Creator makes the whole world happen. This is a unique kind of causing, replicated nowhere else, because it creates all other kinds of causes. In view of this action, Aquinas called God the primary cause. This is the ultimate cause of all other causes without which no other causes would exist.

In bringing the world into being, the loving Creator, acting as primary cause, gifts creatures with their own agency. They become little causes in their own right, having effects on other things. They can be called secondary causes.

As Aquinas figures it, God's action is different from created action. There is an absolute distinction between God who is the primary cause and creatures who are secondary causes in their own particular circumstances of time and space. The primary cause is not the first of a series of causes belonging on the same level as secondary causes. Primary and secondary causes operate on completely different levels (itself an inadequate comparison), one being the active wellspring of all causes and the other participating in the power to cause as things that are burning participate in the power of fire.

With this clue, we can begin to think how it is that the creative activity of God goes forward in and through the working of secondary causes. God's creative purpose is achieved in the course of time in and through the free play of the world's own natural processes. The living mystery of God is so magnificent (pure aliveness, *esse*) and so self-giving in love that there is no threat to divinity in allowing creatures the fullest measure of agency according to their own nature. To the contrary, it is characteristic of the creative power of God to raise up creatures who participate in being to such a degree that they are also creative in their own right.

Good governance

An appeal to best practices of governing helped Aquinas make the point. Those forms of governing are best, he figured, that communicate a higher perfection to the governed. Now there is more excellence in a thing's being a cause in relation to others than in not being a cause. Consequently, God governs in such a way as to empower creatures to be causes toward others. Indeed, "if God were to govern alone, the capacity to be causes would be missing from creatures," to the detriment of their flourishing and their Creator's glory. For it shows more power to give others the power to be effective agents than to do everything oneself.

The wonderful word *concursus*, meaning flowing or running together, comes into play to express this idea. Far from being merely a tool, an instrument, or a puppet in divine hands, the world acts with its own free integrity to shape its own becoming. It is empowered to do so by the transcendent mystery of the Spirit of God, who pervades the world, quickening it to life and gifting creatures with finite agency. Rather than forcing us to choose between divine agency and the agency of the world, this view of creation fosters a both/and sensibility. It provides a technical way of interpreting how mature Love acts while the world evolves according to its own natural laws. *Laudato Si'* stands in this tradition when it states clearly that "God is intimately present to each being without impinging on the autonomy of the creature" (*LS* 80). A view to the contrary would diminish not only creatures but also their Creator.

Both/and

Aquinas, of course, had no notion of an expanding universe filled with galaxies or of the evolution of species on one planet revolving around one star in one of those galaxies. But his work on causes provides a key that allows us to receive scientific discoveries about the world with gratitude. Denis Edwards makes the point succinctly:

> Thomas Aquinas long ago clarified that God's way of acting in the world (what can be called primary causality) is not opposed to the whole network of cause and effect in nature (secondary causality). God's work is achieved in and through creaturely cause and effect. It is not in competition with it. Aquinas never knew Darwin's theory of evolution, but he would have had no difficulty in understanding it as the way that God creates.

In, with, and under nature's own processes, God continuously creates the world. Correlatively, the natural world freely partners the Giver of life in the work of creation, moving through changing time with the integrity of natural processes. God brings into being a universe endowed with its own innate creativity.

It seems to me that it is so easy to forget this, slipping God into the web of interactions as though the divine were simply a bigger and better secondary cause. But the distinction between primary and secondary causes enables thought to hold firm to the mystery of the greatness of God and the free play of natural forces in equal measure, since, to put it bluntly, they are simply not the same thing.

Infinite wellspring of life, God creates the world by empowering the world to make itself. The rigorous distinction between the Creator who is sheer aliveness and all else which receives the power to act intends, rightly, to place the Creator beyond any category commensurate with creatures. God is not a being among other beings, not a secondary cause within the functioning of the world. The very fact that the Creator gives be-ing to everything in every place means that the living God cannot be ranked with any other particular factor or included in any list of finite causes. Rather, the Giver of life vivifies, pervades, and surrounds all things as their dynamic source, present empowerment, and ineffable goal. The living God who is "over all and through all and in all" (Eph 4:6) makes it all possible. The distinction between primary and secondary causes offers one way to think about this.

It is well to remember that the magnificent creative relationship between God and the world cannot be understood without remainder. In love the Giver of life freely and generously invests nature with the power to organize itself and emerge into ever-new, more complex forms, and to do so according to its own ways of operating. All the while, the indwelling Creator Spirit continuously empowers and accompanies the evolving world through its history of shaping and breaking apart, birthing and perishing, hitting dead ends and finding new avenues into the future.

Let us ponder this relationship until it becomes impossible to say the word "God" without appreciating how the Creator Spirit moves throughout the Earth with compassionate love that grants nature its own creative integrity and humans their own freedom, all the while companioning them through the terror of history toward a future, promised but unknown.

The earth is full of the steadfast love of God.

—Psalm 33:5

12

The author of beauty

From the greatness and the beauty of created things
their original author, by analogy, is seen.
—Wisdom 13:5

In one of the most engaging book introductions I have ever read, Ed Yong starts *An Immense World* with a thought experiment. Imagine a spacious room with an actual weighty elephant in it. A mouse scurries in. A robin hops alongside it. An owl perches on a beam. A bat hangs upside down. A rattlesnake slithers along the floor. A spider spins a web. A mosquito buzzes. A bumblebee sits on a potted sunflower. And a curious human named Rebecca walks about. In broad strokes Yong begins to describe how each perceives the presence of the other. They smell through trunk, tongue, antennae and nose. Some hear sonic pitches too high or low to be audible to anyone else. They see colors differently, the ultraviolet bullseye at the center of the sunflower visible to the bird and the bee but not to the others. Some are exquisitely tuned to sense vibrations when others move. Some, like the mosquito, feel radiation from other bodies' warmth. The bird feels the attraction of Earth's magnetic field pointing it south, now that colder days are propelling migration, and heads for the window. Rebecca cannot hear the high mouse squeaks or the low elephant rumbles, but listens to the robin singing though her ears cannot pick out all the tune's complexities.

All these creatures, Yong writes, "share the same physical space but experience it in wildly and wondrously different ways." The same holds true across the planet:

> Earth teems with sights and textures, sounds and vibrations, smells and tastes, electric and magnetic fields. But every animal can only tap into a small fraction of reality's fullness. Each is enclosed within its own unique sensory bubble, perceiving but a tiny sliver of an immense world.

What a magnificence! Untold species living the arc of their lives with different sensations of the physical world and interacting with that world and each other for better or worse.

The description of these animals all sensing the world differently brings to mind one philosopher's exclamation:

> What must the "personality" or "character" be like of a Creator in whose image this astounding universe of ours is made. . . . Must not the "personality" of such a Creator be one charged not only with unfathomable power and energy, but also with dazzling imaginative creativity?

When discussing a work of art such as a painting, a song, a novel, a film, or a creative invention such as the light bulb or the iPhone, people commonly assume that something of the creator of the piece is reflected in the finished work. Look at how those brushstrokes reflect Van Gogh's tormented mind. Listen to how the Black experience of suffering and resilience resounds in that jazz piece. What a keen intuition Steve Jobs had to envision such a user-friendly design for a new kind of phone that connects to the web. With a thousand precautions, the same holds true for personal influence on other human beings. Parenting, teaching, coaching, mentoring, working with people in any field: when human actions influence the becoming of someone else, the imprint of our own values and style filters through. There is never an exact one-to-one correspondence, but we do leave our fingerprints.

Biblical wisdom writers applied this same logic to the natural world, the work of God's hands: "From the greatness and the beauty of created things, their original author, by analogy, is seen" (Wis 13:5). The world's magnificence reveals something about the Creator who gifts it with its own natural existence. There is never an exact correspondence, hence "by analogy," but the world with its greatness and beauty does offer a glimpse. It can teach those who have eyes to see and ears to hear.

Stopping short

The wisdom writer who penned the lines at the heading of this meditation was worried about people who appreciated the magnificence of the world but stopped there. These folks were foolish because while they were awed by the beautiful things they saw, they failed to go one step further and recognize the artisan behind them. Worse yet, some even made natural wonders into gods in their own right. The whole passage lays out a lucid logic of creation:

> They were unable from the good things that are
>   seen to know the one who exists,
> nor did they recognize the artisan while paying
>   heed to the works;

> but they supposed that either fire or wind or swift air
> or the circle of the stars or turbulent water
> or the luminaries of heaven were the gods that rule
>   the world.
> If through delight in the beauty of these things
>   people assumed them to be gods,
> let them know how much better than these is their
>   Maker,
> for the author of beauty created them.
> And if people were amazed at their power and working,
> let them perceive how much more powerful is the
>   one who formed them.
> For from the greatness and beauty of created things
>   their original author, by analogy, is seen.
>   (Wis 13:1–5)

This writer does show some empathy. Perhaps people stop short "because the things that are seen are so beautiful" (13:7). They surely are. But the beauty of the shining stars and planets in the night sky; the strength of fire, wind, and turbulent water—none of these are gods. Look again, people, and don't be ignorant! Let your spirit keep going and get to the source, the author of beauty.

A SACRAMENTAL IMAGINATION

There is a connection between this view of creation and thinking with a sacramental imagination. Very broadly, the term sacrament refers to a gesture, word, or object that represents something good and holy and communicates it in some way. You might think of the holy nourishment Bessie gave to Franny in J. D. Salinger's novel *Franny and Zooey.* Her brother Zooey tells her: "How in hell are you going to recognize a legitimate holy man when you see one if you don't even know a cup of consecrated chicken soup when it's right in front of your nose?" Franny is lacking the sense to see the soup as a sacrament of Bessie's care.

In the Christian tradition sacraments are ritual actions of the church that use words and simple material things like water, oil, bread, and wine to communicate God's saving love to persons. In the ecclesial setting, each is like a cup of consecrated soup. Persons are healed, nourished and strengthened by these communal acts performed in the name and spirit of Christ to go forward to be better lovers of God and the dear neighbor.

Robust creation faith sees that these ritual actions also illuminate the presence of a broader sacramental dynamic at work throughout the cosmos. The Creator Spirit makes what is physical —stars, planets, soil, water, air, plants, animals, humans, ecological habitats—and, more mobile than any motion, continuously breathes them into existence. Pervaded and encircled by the Creator Spirit, Earth is a physical place of extravagant dynamism that bodies forth the presence and activity of God. In its own way it is a sacrament, the primordial sacrament. From the greatness and the beauty of created things the author of beauty can be seen.

Pregnant with surprise

The evolving Earth in an expanding universe is, of course, not finished. In seeking God through the beauty of what has been created, we need to bear two cautions in mind.

First, the correspondence between the world and God is indirect. The biblical wisdom writer knew this. The words "by analogy" make us aware that the Creator cannot be simply equated with the world's finite beauty but as its Maker is always ever greater. In our day, scientific knowledge of cosmic and biological development spells this out clearly. We know that the world's gorgeous design has not been executed by divine agency, as we might imagine a single person drawing up a blue print and directing matters from above. Rather, it is the result of innumerable natural processes and, in terms of life, of small adaptations of creatures to their environment, a design from below, so to speak. Many changes occur randomly. Some adaptations are successful in the current environment and thus filter through to the next generation; some make the organism unfit and so die out; but none are predictable. The array of creatures in the opening room of Yong's *Immense World* exists thanks to these processes. So too does the beauty of Earth today in its oceans and varied landscapes. "By analogy" is key.

Second, in view of the future fullness yet to come, theologian John Haught wisely cautions against settling down with an uncritical view of the natural world as a sacrament or a sacred place. This view can be static and get closed in on itself. With its emphasis on beauty it tends to ignore the massive suffering and death that are ever-present companions. With its emphasis on the present moment it tends to overlook the promise of what is yet to come. As Haught colorfully puts it, the whole of evolution teaches that from the beginning the world was "seeded with promise," "pregnant with surprise." And it is not over yet.

Still, in a secular culture that assumes the world is just a given, not a gift, tracing links from the world's beauty to its author has a profoundly beneficial effect. Instead of feeding a utilitarian attitude that promotes using up the world as we wish without a thought for future generations, it awakens an attitude of reverence. The practice of seeing this gorgeous world reflecting its author inspires us to honor its intrinsic worth and invigorates energy for its care, all the way into the future. Not incidentally, it also bonds us closer to the author of all this beauty.

Let this wisdom dynamic have its way with your spirit. Take a moment to gaze at something beautiful. Enjoy it. Wonder what makes it so attractive. Let its beauty carry you into the presence of the author of beauty.

> *Ever since the creation of the world God's eternal power and divine nature, invisible though they are, have been seen and understood through the things God has made.*
>
> —Romans 1:20

Jesus and the Earth

13

Messianic peace

He was with the wild animals.
—Mark 1:13

Each of the four gospels in the New Testament begins by giving the reader a heads-up that what follows is a story of good news about Jesus who is the anointed one, the expected Messiah, the Christ. They all make the point by using the testimony of John the baptizer. Apart from that, the ways they inform the reader are colorfully different. Luke employs an angel's annunciation to Mary, a trip to Bethlehem, and angels in the night sky singing to shepherds keeping watch. Matthew brings in a genealogy, an angel's annunciation to Joseph, and magi who arrive bearing gifts after following a star and asking directions. John writes a prologue dense with theological themes, starting with the Word of God active in creation who became flesh and dwelt among us. And Mark? Uniquely among the gospels, Mark signals Jesus's identity as Messiah by posing him with the wild animals.

The first of the gospels to be written, Mark has no stories of Jesus' birth, no mention of parents in a stable, no shepherds, no angels, no magi. It opens with John clothed in camel's hair baptizing crowds of people in the Jordan River. Into this scene steps the adult Jesus of Nazareth. After he, too, is baptized, the skies open. The Spirit descends upon him like a dove and a voice from heaven declares, "You are my beloved Son; with you I am well pleased" (Mark 1:11). Right afterward he heads for a desolate wilderness where he is tempted by Satan.

Details of the baptism scene may well be familiar from other gospels. But then Mark inserts a singular scene. After resisting Satan in the wilderness and before receiving the care of angels, Jesus "was with the wild animals." What an interesting picture! Rarely depicted in art, hardly ever used as a text for preaching, and almost never included in theological discussions about Christ's identity or mission, the scene has a certain pride of place at the very beginning of Mark's Gospel. How does it reveal that Jesus is the Christ and what does this indicate about creation?

The Wolf and the Lamb

Jewish hope for redemption included all of creation. This inclusive, expectant tradition passed into the early Christian community without question or dispute. As Mark's Gospel opens, the baptismal scene with John's testimony, the dove, and the voice from heaven makes crystal clear to the reader that Jesus is the Messiah. Continuing the work of identifying Jesus, Mark places him in the desert with dangerous beasts. The motif "he was with the wild animals" has tremendous symbolic resonance. Jesus establishes a relationship with wild animals that enacts in an anticipatory way the harmony between all creatures that is part of the hope for the coming messianic age.

Behind this scene lies the biblical tradition of future peace between all contentious creatures, humans and animals alike, within their own kind and among one another. One wonderful oracle of Isaiah portrays the coming reign of the messiah as an era of such deep peace that wild animals and domestic animals and human children will dwell together without fearing harm, not even for the most vulnerable young among them. Note the use of words like lamb, kid, calf, and child that refer to the youngsters of various species in this oracle:

> The wolf shall live with the lamb; the leopard shall lie
> down with the kid;
> the calf and the lion will feed together, and a little
> child shall lead them.
> The cow and the bear shall graze; their young shall lie
> down together;
> and the lion shall eat straw like the ox.
> The nursing child shall play over the hole of the asp,
> and the weaned child shall put its hand on the
> adder's den.
> They will not hurt or destroy on all my holy mountain,
> For the earth will be full of the knowledge of the Lord
> as the waters cover the sea. (Isa 11:6–9)

By means of the motif of Jesus's peaceable presence with the wild animals, Mark wants the reader to know that the messianic age is beginning.

Being with

In the first century the Judean wilderness included the following wild animals: bears, leopards, wolves, scorpions, hyenas, jackals, wild boars, and poisonous snakes such as cobras and vipers. Any one of them could kill you. But in Mark's scene there is no sense of danger from the ferocious beasts. Neither is there any domination or domestication from the human side. There is no hostility between animals and human, no violence in any direction. Instead Jesus is *with* the animals, a word that elsewhere has a strong positive sense of close association or friendship. Recall, for example, how when Jesus was on trial a maid saw Peter warming himself by the fire and said, “You also were with Jesus, the man from Nazareth” (Mark 14:67). You were with him means you are part of his group, you are one of his disciples. In Mark’s scene Jesus and the animals are there “with” each other, together in mutual companionship. Such peaceable company offers a glimpse of the promised eschatological future when enmity and threat among creatures will be healed. With Jesus’s advent, the hope-for future is at hand.

Though sadly neglected, this christic image has untapped potential for an age of ecological crisis. It offers a compelling resource for people to develop a living faith in which relationship with Christ does not exclude but includes hope for the rest of God’s creatures. As biblical scholar Richard Bauckham observes:

> For us Jesus’s companionable presence with the wild animals affirms their independent value for themselves and for God. He does not adopt them into the human world but lets them be themselves in peace, leaving them their wilderness, affirming them as creatures who share the world with us in the community of God’s creation.

Jesus does not terrorize or control the wild animals or make them pets. They do not fear him, attack him, submit to him, or serve him. The real beauty of the word “with,” Bauckham suggests, is that it gives us a warrant to follow Jesus by living as sisters and brothers with animals, our fellow creatures who have their own destiny. Thereby we can experience the grace of otherness which God offers us in the diversity of animal creation, which is missed when animals are reduced to usefulness or threat. Thanks to this grace we are impelled to develop wholesome ecological relationships with animals and act vigorously for their well-being, which includes protecting the habitats they need to live.

Let us sit for a while with this scene. Imagine if it began to be depicted in paintings, stained glass windows, catechisms, holy cards, hymns. It would be hard to ignore the ecological dimension of Jesus's mission, or to forget the redemptive hope for all of groaning creation that his life, death, and resurrection promise.

> *[Jesus] said to them, "Go into the whole world and proclaim the gospel to every creature."*
>
> —Mark 16:15

14

Salvation is on its way from God!

God reigns! Let the earth rejoice;
let the many islands be glad.
—Psalm 97:1

GOOD NEWS!

"Now after John was arrested, Jesus came to Galilee proclaiming the good news of God" (Mark 1:14). The public ministry of Jesus was a marvel. Lasting only a brief time, his preaching and powerfully kind actions made such an impression that after his death and resurrection people remembered. They passed on memories of his words and deeds orally and then wrote them down as gospels, which reach through the centuries to inspire lives and shape communities to this day. Like any public, prophetic figure whose words and deeds have an impact, Jesus was on fire with a mission. If you ask about the center of gravity of his ministry, the pivot around which everything else circled, it would be the good news that God was drawing near to save.

All three synoptic gospels portray Jesus expressing this good news through the ancient biblical symbol of the reign or the rule or the kingdom of God. For Mark the good news of God is that "the reign of God has come near" (1:15). Matthew calls it "the good news of the kingdom" (4:23). Luke depicts Jesus' urgency: "I must proclaim the good news of the kingdom of God" (4:43) from town to town. The symbol is rooted in the precious and all too rare experience of a realm of peace and plenty ruled by a sovereign who ensures that all will thrive.

But the world is not as it should be. The treacherous deal treacherously, as the prophet Isaiah lamented. Horrendous war, hatred, murder, racism, sexual violence, corruption among the powerful, unjust judgments meted out to the poor, economic poverty, squalor and misery, oppression and injustice lie in every direction; rivers dried up, land lying waste, animals crying out for water—the world is not big enough to contain the books that would be needed to give a full account of the suffering that rolls on and on, with death over all. The coming of God's reign promises regime change:

> Let the heavens be glad, and the earth rejoice;
> let the sea and what fills it resound;
> let the plains be joyful and all that is in them.
> Then shall all the trees of the forest rejoice
> before the saving God who comes,
> who comes to govern the earth,
> To govern the world with justice
> and the peoples with faithfulness.
> (Ps 96:11–13)

Notice that the coming of the kingdom of God brings justice, of the strong and trustworthy kind that elicits joy. Notice, too, the intertwining of the natural world and people in the joyful justice of God's reign. Jesus drank deeply from the waters of this symbol. Giving a legacy that lasts to this day, he taught his disciples to pray, "thy kingdom come." Let us ponder Jesus's ministry through the lens of the reign of God, which is cosmic in scope.

A DIFFICULTY

In our day the symbol of the kingdom of God has a hard time engendering enthusiasm. A kingdom seems to smack of a one-way exercise of authority, inherited privilege, colonial oppression, imperial violence, and patriarchal rule. The suggestion that we speak instead of the "kin-dom of God" meets with approval in many circles, and even relief. Kin-dom in this context stands for a liberating gathering of mutual brothers and sisters in a beloved community working for love and justice. In my view, a wide use of the term kin-dom of God would bring many benefits, especially if we brought creatures who are not human into the picture as our kin in the community of creation.

The kingdom of God may not resonate in our current milieu, and for good reasons. Given the importance of the symbol in the gospels and its daily repetition in the *Lord's Prayer*, however, I do think it is important to appreciate what it means in its own context. The point to ponder here is that Jesus used the term as it came to him from centuries of Jewish tradition where the coming of the reign of God, the Creator and Lover of heaven and earth, meant the defeat of evil.

To open up the possibility of understanding, I have given students the project of picturing what the world would look like if the kingdom of God actually came for just one day. You may want to take a moment to try this yourself. Their short essays reflect a better world seen through young eyes. There would be no more rape; no more school shootings; no more murder; an end to prejudice against LGBTQ persons; respect for people of every race; no more war; peace throughout the world; enough money for food, with no more world hunger, and with pizza and ice cream for all; no refugees; no cancer; no one addicted to drugs; parents loving their children; no one failing a course (!); social media filled with positive vibes; the Bronx River fit for fish and recreation; logging in the Amazon stopped; all species thriving; the planet cooling off; and on and on. It is hard to imagine such a plenitude of goodness. But the symbol of God's reign holds the promise of blessing for all.

A paraphrase

Aware of the difficulties that cluster around kingdom language in our day, Dutch theologian Edward Schillebeeckx has proposed a lovely paraphrase for contemporary ears. When we hear Jesus proclaiming "The kingdom of God has come near!", we should hear him say, "Salvation is on its way from God!" Since the Creator of heaven and earth is gracious and merciful, indeed a liberating God of compassion with a heart for justice, this can mean only freedom, healing, the end of sorrow, and good winning over evil throughout the whole of creation. This is the good news Jesus is urgently bringing to public attention.

In response to the announcement that the kingdom of God is near, Jesus called for his listeners to "repent." This means something more than the usual connection with guilt, shame, and sorrow for sin. In this context it resounds with the challenge to listen up! Change your heart! Turn your mind around! Convert your spirit to what is happening! Wake up to this good news! Be open to this coming blessing! It is all so joyful.

Savor the rich description of God's reign flowing through Psalm 146 and see if you can feel some of its attractive power:

> Happy are those whose hope is in the Lord their God,
> who made the heavens and the earth, the seas and
> all that is in them;

who is faithful forever;
who brings about justice for the oppressed,
who gives food to the hungry;
who sets prisoners free;
who opens the eyes of the blind;
who lifts up those who are bowed down;
who loves the righteous;
who protects strangers;
who upholds the orphan and the widow, but brings the
way of the wicked to ruin. God will reign forever.

There is such a sense of wholeness in the symbol of God's reign. Salvation is on its way from God! It is precisely because the Creator loves the world that divine care extends throughout the human and natural world to reach the least of creatures who are in trouble. This is what love does. The identification of God who creates with God who is merciful and comes to redeem is bedrock in the scriptures. The natural world and human beings within it are all connected, and we will all flourish together when God reigns.

In word and deed

The motif of God's saving reign drawing near served as the backbone of Jesus's ministry. It resounds through his parables, many of which begin "The kingdom of God is like . . ." The reign of God is precisely *not* like the Roman Empire, which conquers with violence, imposes its will, demands crushing taxes, crucifies people and makes them suffer. To the contrary. It is like seed scattered on the ground that sprouts into nourishing grain even when the farmer is not looking. It is like a tiny mustard seed that grows to be a great shrub sheltering the birds; like yeast that leavens a whole batch of dough once a woman mixes it in; like seed sown in good soil that brings forth a hundred-fold yield at harvest. The stories use occurrences in the natural world to point to something quite wonderful coming to pass, something thrilling and unexpected, with a bit of the uncanny at work.

In the spirit of the good news of God's reign drawing near, Jesus' actions gave foretastes of its goodness. He healed the sick, fed crowds of hungry people, taught multitudes about the centrality of love and mercy, looked upon nature with a loving eye, shared joyful meals with tax collectors and sinners, attended especially to those on the margins, and argued with religious leaders who resisted this compassionate vision, all while seeking moments of quiet prayer. His ministry cut a swath of goodness through a troubled time. The God of his heart was the Creator of heaven and earth, and everything was encompassed in the transformation he envisioned.

Even death

Salvation is on its way from God! As Jesus proclaimed it, a sense that God's reign is dawning gave rise to a little surge of hope. To this day it can rouse people from despair. We pray "thy kingdom come" in hope that this good news will appear even now in bright spots of peace, justice, and the healing of creation while history is still under way, and one fine day when God's faithful love will reign throughout the whole world once and for all. The prophet Isaiah filled this symbol with an astounding final hope:

> On this mountain God who reigns will make for all
> peoples
> a feast of rich food, a feast of well-aged wines,
> of rich food filled with marrow, of well-aged wines
> strained clear.

And on this mountain God will destroy
  the shroud that is cast over all peoples,
  the covering that is spread over all nations;
God will swallow up death forever,
  and will wipe away the tears from all faces.
    (Isa 25:7–8)

Wiping away tears from someone's face is such a tender gesture. Lovers do this, as do good parents with their little ones. "See, this is our God," Isaiah continues. The day is coming when God's reign will defeat even death throughout all creation. It is beyond good news.

For your strength does not depend on numbers nor your might on the powerful. But you are the God of the lowly, helper of the oppressed, upholder of the weak, protector of the forsaken, savior of those without hope. Please, please, God of my ancestors, God of the heritage of Israel, God of heaven and earth, Creator of the waters, Ruler of all your creation, hear my prayer!

—Judith 9:11–12

15
The gaze of Jesus

Consider the lilies of the field, how they grow; they neither toil nor spin, yet I tell you, not even Solomon in all his glory was clothed like one of these.

—Matthew 6:28–29

An angle of vision

Consider how Jesus looked upon the world of nature. He noticed a field of wildflowers, little plants not specially cultivated but just growing naturally where they happened to take root. They were insignificant on the grand stage of world events. But they were gorgeous! Captivated by their beauty, he recognized their generous Source. Reflecting further, he saw that the flowers gave human beings a reason to trust in God in the midst of anxiety. If God so clothed the grass of the field, which is alive today and tomorrow is thrown into the oven, don't you think God will clothe you too? In fact, even more so? Where is your faith? A true wisdom teacher, Jesus drew an important lesson for human life from a few transitory flowers cared for by God. Where does this kind of seeing come from?

It comes from the creation theology of the Jewish religious tradition. As a member of the Jewish people, Jesus was heir to this teaching. Born and raised in an observant household and a practicing Jew all his life, he learned this tradition which shaped his awareness of the world and gave him a bedrock upon which to stand. The God of his heart was the creating God of Genesis who made heaven and earth and all their blooming, buzzing array of creatures. This same ineffable holy mystery was the rainbow God who covenanted with every creature of flesh on the earth, the liberating God of enslaved people, the challenging and compassionate God of the prophets, the engaged God of the psalms praised by everything that has breath, the God of justice and hope who hears the cry of the poor, the God whose care encompasses humans and the cosmos alike. In the biblical view, divine love is all encompassing: God "heals the brokenhearted and binds up their wounds, counts the stars and gives to all their names" (Ps 147:3–4).

Note that in the teaching drawn from wildflowers Jesus does not use the greater capacity of humans in order to make a negative point about flowers. His argument presupposes that humans and flowers are all creatures of God. Not having imbibed the Greek philosophical notion of the hierarchy of being, it would not have occurred to him to separate out human beings from the natural world and consider the flowers of little religious importance. Human beings are clearly valued and loved by God, but as creatures who are part of the whole beloved creation.

The lay of the land

As is true of humans generally, Jesus' way of looking at the world was concretely influenced by the type of environment in which he lived. In his case this was mostly rural countryside rather than urban or suburban surroundings.

He spent most of his childhood and adult life in the small farming village of Nazareth, a poor place situated in the fertile district of Galilee. Blessed by weather conducive to a long growing season and rich harvests, the land was dotted with vineyards, wheat fields, pastures, and orchards of olive, fig, and other fruit trees. To the east the land sank down toward the Sea of Galilee, a deep freshwater lake with a goodly population of fish. Throughout Galilee the majority of people engaged in agriculture, while some fished or tended flocks, and still others engaged in crafts like carpentry that served the needs of those workers. Despite the rich natural environment, people were economically stressed due to debt and taxation practices imposed by the Roman Empire.

Coming as he did from such an agrarian setting, it is little wonder Jesus's parables are salted with references to seeds and harvests, wheat and weeds, vineyards and fig trees, rain and sunsets, sheep and nesting birds. He also gleaned examples to illustrate his parables from human ways of making a living on the land, such as farming, herding sheep, growing wheat and making bread, growing grapes and making wine, and cultivating trees.

A search of the gospels turns up the following animals mentioned in Jesus's sayings and parables: birds (dove, eagle, raven, sparrow, vulture), camel, chickens (rooster, mother hen, chicks), dog, donkey, fish, fox, gnat, goat, moth, ox, pig, scorpion, sheep, snake, viper, and wolf. He also referenced a multitude of plants: bramble, fig tree, grape vine, herbs (mint, dill, cumin, rue), mulberry tree, mustard plant, reed, thorn, weed, wheat, and wildflowers. He drew points from the west wind that brings rain, the southern wind that brings heat, and sunsets that predict the next day's weather. Urban dwellers may well find the idea of this much ordinary exposure to the natural world daunting. The point is that Jesus saw it all as God's world.

Suffering and Death

Inhabiting biblical faith in God the Creator, Jesus had a tangible and loving relationship with the natural world. He looked upon nature with fondness and wonder and admired its beauty. But he was no romantic. Gazing with compassion on the way life actually happens, he also saw that it was a place of struggle, suffering, and death.

Here were birds for sale in a market, which closed off the possibility of their ever flying free again; they would no doubt end up as someone's supper. A tough situation for the birds. But as Jesus saw it, this did not free them from God's loving care:

Are not two sparrows sold for a penny? Yet not one of them falls to the ground without your heavenly father knowing it. (Matt 10:29). Or as Luke's gospel puts it, "Yet not one of them is forgotten in God's sight" (12:6). Sparrows are the cheapest birds in the market. Like wildflowers in a field, they are of little consequence in the human scheme of things. Yet even death cannot separate them from the love of God who created them. The relationship of creation ensures that the Giver of life does not lose track of any creature, not even of one little bird lying dead on the ground. Believing this, Jesus drew an important lesson for stressed-out human beings. The same Creator also knows you intimately, to the point of numbering the hairs on your head; do not be afraid; you are worth more than many sparrows.

The encouragement to trust in God is certainly the key point of this saying of Jesus. In an era of ecological awareness, what stands out just as strongly is Jesus's assurance of God's care for the least of flying birds.

To the peripheries

The gaze of Jesus which noticed a field of wildflowers and a pair of sparrows for sale in the market also looked upon human beings with interested love. It is striking how the gospels depict him noticing people on the margins of a cultural group, those who, like wildflowers and sparrows, could be dismissed as of little account. Even when not asked, he saw how an individual person was suffering and was moved with compassion to act. What happened one day in the synagogue is typical:

> Now he was teaching in one of the synagogues on the Sabbath. And just then there appeared a woman with a spirit that had crippled her for eighteen years. She was bent over and was quite unable to stand up straight. When Jesus saw her, he called her over and said, "Woman, you are set free from your ailment." When he laid his hands on her, immediately she stood up straight and began praising God. (Luke 13:1–13)

It would be understandable if Jesus had not noticed this bent-over woman at all. With her crooked back forcing her own eyes to stay focused on the ground, she did not look at him or try to gain his attention. Arriving late for the sabbath service, she slipped in at the back of the congregation. Meanwhile he was holding forth as that day's special public speaker in front of the gathered community, no doubt concentrating on what he wanted to say next. He was a strong, healthy man in an honored position of authority. She was a crippled woman of little use to society.

But his gaze traveled to the periphery. As Luke writes, "Jesus saw her." He interrupted his teaching to bring her forward and heal her. While she praised God, he had to deal with the indignant criticism of the community's leader for healing on the sabbath. With quick wit he rebutted the leader's disapproval. Don't you untie your ox or donkey and lead them to water for a drink even on the sabbath? Why should this daughter of Abraham not also be untied from the bonds of her infirmity? His opponents were silenced. The people rejoiced. It's a great story.

The point to consider is that the gaze of Jesus was compassionate, a kind of seeing with the heart, not utilitarian. As with the wildflowers and the sparrows, he saw the worth of this woman as a beloved creature of God and acted to communicate God's care, as best he was able. It would have been so easy not to see her.

Time and again Jesus's deeply religious, kindly way of turning his gaze toward the periphery creates new possibilities. Consider one more incident. We might expect that this teacher, or anyone for that matter, walking along a road with a boisterous crowd would keep his attention on the pressing crush of people at street level. But a short, despised tax collector ripe for conversion had climbed a tree.

> When Jesus came to the place, he looked up and said to him, "Zacchaeus, hurry and come down, for I must stay at your house today." (Luke 19:5)

"He looked up." The resulting change of heart made life better not only for the tax man but also for so many other needy people whom he had cheated. They got back a bonanza, the money he had wrongly taken from them multiplied by four. A heap of criticism, however, was laid on Jesus's head because "he has gone to be the guest of one who is a sinner." That criticism followed Jesus around like a toxic cloud. He was a friend of tax collectors and sinners and even ate at the same table, a sign of intimate bonding in Middle Eastern culture. Nevertheless, the gaze of Jesus saw such publicly ostracized people as beloved creatures of God. With that vision he channeled God's love to them through his own presence. They might be lost, but his mission was to seek and save, not to condemn.

Jesus gazed upon people with love. When a rich young man who had observed the commandments sought instruction about how to live an even better life, "Jesus, looking at him, loved him" (Mark 10:21). There was so much potential in this person! Although the advice Jesus offered was sadly refused, his gaze of love did not turn to hate.

The gaze of love also impelled Jesus to look upon some people with justified anger. When religious leaders watched to see if he would heal on the sabbath, placing their own narrow interpretation of the law above the good of someone who was suffering, "He looked around at them with anger; he was grieved at their hardness of heart and said to the man, 'Stretch out your hand.' He stretched it out, and his hand was restored" (Mark 3:5).

Jesus's way of seeing could actually create new relationships among disparate people. Once when he was teaching in a crowded house, word came that some members of his family were outside asking to see him. "And looking at those who sat around him, he said, 'Here are my mother and my brothers! Whoever does the will of God is brother and sister and mother to me'" (Mark 3:33–35). Jesus could see in the people packed into that room a new kind of family coming into being, one not based on ties of blood or tribal allegiance, but on responsiveness to God. All are held in affection by God who creates and saves the world. In that light he could recognize strangers who loved God as his own siblings, and those who nurture life in others as his own mother. They could look upon each other in like manner and become a force for good in the suffering world.

One God, one world

What would it be like if we emulated the gaze of Jesus? Try it. Try looking at the world with his kind of regard. The whole cosmos would come clear as God's beloved creation. The natural world down to its least member would appear as a wonder. We would appreciate its beauty, learn from it, care for it with vigor, oppose its destruction, and use it with respect. Our attention would turn toward the peripheries where human needs abound. We would catch sight of the bent-over woman in our own circles, the ostracized man in the tree, the searching youth. We would see and be rightfully angered by injustice rather than ignore or deny its brutality. We would recognize our kin in lovers of God of all kinds. We are all on creation's journey to fullness of life—flowers of the field, birds of the air, suffering, sinning, seeking humans of the most diverse ecosystems, everything.

> *Look at the birds of the air: they neither sow nor reap nor gather into barns, and yet your heavenly father feeds them.*
>
> —Matthew 6:26

16

Born of a woman: God with us, the kangaroos, the grasses, the soil

The Word was made flesh and dwelt among us.
—John 1:14

Every new creature who emerges into life onto this planet, whether from egg, womb or seed, is a moving point of intersection between the past and the future. Each new life carries a genetic imprint evolved by its ancestors over millions of years. It also bears a rich promise of how this heritage will play out in the as-yet unforeseen circumstances of its own time on Earth. Writing of human births, the philosopher Martin Buber expressed this with eloquence:

> In every hour the human race begins. We forget this too easily in face of the massive fact of past life, of so-called world history, and of the fact that each child is born with a given biological disposition. . . . Yet in this as in every hour, what has not been invades the structure of what is, with ten thousand countenances, of which not one has been seen before, with ten thousand souls still undeveloped but ready to develop—a creative event if ever there

> was one, newness rising up, primal potential might. This potentiality, streaming unconquered, however much of it is squandered, is the reality *child*: this phenomenon of uniqueness, which is more than just begetting and birth, this grace of beginning again and ever again.

For Christians the birth of one particular child in Bethlehem enacted this grace with amazing strength. Born of a woman and the Hebrew gene pool, Jesus inherited the Jewish tradition's belief in a gracious and merciful Creator and bore it into a future that no one could have imagined. Most details of his historical life are unknown, as is the case with poor, rural people in general. What we do know is that as an adult this first-century Jewish carpenter in Roman-occupied Palestine appeared briefly in the public eye, calling disciples to join him in a traveling ministry that lasted from one to three years. The gospels present a riveting picture of a vibrant person passionately in love with God. He emphasized divine care for all creatures, especially for those who were lost, poor, disparaged, or on the margins of society. It all ended violently, with the political imperial establishment crucifying him as a troubling upstart.

Peculiar to Christianity, what would normally be the end of the story turned unexpectedly into a new beginning. The women and men who formed his band of disciples experienced his presence among them in a new way. Drawing on Jewish expectation of what God would do at the end of the world, they began to understand that the Spirit of God had raised Jesus from the dead into new life. This new act of creation just spun their minds around. It anchored hope for a blessed future for the whole world.

It also triggered reflection about Jesus himself. In the course of the first century the disciples came to believe that in Jesus Christ the unfathomable God of gracious love had personally joined the flesh of the world with its vulnerability and death in order to save from within. In other words, in Jesus God is not only *with* and *for* human beings but is present *as* a human being. Searching the scriptures the disciples found vocabulary to put this belief into words. They began to speak about him as the Messiah or Christ, as Emmanuel or God with us, as the Son of God, the Wisdom of God, the Word of God.

In the beginning

A high point of this development appears in the opening passage of the gospel of John. "In the beginning," the gospel begins (John 1:1). The alert reader hears the first words of the book of Genesis, establishing a link between the story of Jesus and the story of creation. In the beginning, before there was a world, there was the Word, who was with God, who was God; this was the Word through whom all things were made, who bore life and light for all. Having established the divine creating and saving character of the Word of God, the prologue reaches its high point with a bold assertion: "And the Word was made flesh and dwelt among us" (John 1:14). It is an extraordinary claim. God's personal self-expression, the Word, full of loving-kindness and faithfulness, joined the living material flesh of the created world.

Read at the Catholic liturgy every Christmas day, this text expresses what would come to be called the incarnation (from the Latin *carne*, flesh), the belief that the living God who is utterly beyond comprehension has joined the flesh of Earth in one particular human being of one limited time and place. The verb usually translated as "dwelt" or "lived" among us is also ably translated as "pitched a tent," as in the tent in the wilderness where God's presence dwelt and traveled with the Hebrew people after their escape from slavery (Exod 33:7–11). Now, in the person of Jesus, God's self-expressing word pitched a tent in the midst of the world, becoming part of its history.

It is important to note that the gospel does not say the Word became a human being (Greek *anthropos*), or a male person (Greek *aner*), but flesh (Greek *sarx*), a broader reality. Sarx or flesh connotes the finite quality of the bodily, material world which, while beautiful, is also fragile, vulnerable, prone to trouble and sin, and perishable, the very opposite of divine majesty. A reader with allegiance to the Greek dualistic philosophy that opposed spirit to matter would be horrified at the thought of divinity being contaminated by matter in this way. In fact, the first Christian heresy actually denied the reality of Jesus's body. It held that his body only appeared to be real flesh; he did not take on human flesh from the Virgin Mary but passed through her womb the way water passes through a tube, remaining a different substance. No contamination from matter for him.

By contrast, German theologian Karl Rahner asserts the meaning of the gospel bluntly, leaving no wiggle room: "The statement of God's *Incarnation*—of God's becoming *material*—*is* the most basic statement of Christology." Taking the powerful biblical theme of God's dwelling among the people of Israel a step further, John's gospel affirms that in a new and saving event the Word of God *became* flesh, entered personally into the sphere of the material world to shed light on all from within.

Odd as it may seem to others, and sometimes even to themselves, Christians hold the belief, wildly radical on the face of it, that in Jesus Christ the ineffable, self-expressing God joined the world in the flesh, acquired a genuine human personal story, even an agonizing death, and did so as a participant in the history of life on our planet. God joined our mess, as one of my students put it.

All flesh

This may be good news for human beings, but what could it possibly mean for the ecological world of fish and trees and water?

Recall that enfleshed human beings exist as part of an interconnected community. Scientific knowledge today has repositioned the human species as an intrinsic part of the evolutionary network of life on our planet, which in turn is a part of the solar system, which itself came into being as a later chapter of cosmic history. The landscape of our imagination expands when we realize that human connection to nature is so deep that we can no longer completely define human identity without including the grand sweep of cosmic history and our shared biological ancestry in the community of life on this planet. This colorful example from Charles Darwin makes the point well:

> What can be more curious than that the hand of a man formed for grasping, that of a mole for digging, the leg of the horse, the paddle of the porpoise, and the wing of the bat, should all be constructed on the same pattern, and should include the same bones, in the same relative positions?

If one holds the view that God created each species directly, Darwin continues, we can only say that it has pleased the Creator to construct each animal in this way. But if we suppose an ancient progenitor had its limbs arranged this way, then all descendants inherit the pattern. The bones might be enveloped in a thick membrane to form a paddle to swim, or a thin membrane to form a wing, or they might be separated to form fingers and toes, or they may be lengthened or shortened for some other profitable purpose; but there will be no tendency to alter the framework. Indeed, the same names are given to these bones configured the same way in widely different animals. What a grand system, formed by descent with slow, successive modifications!

Human flesh, rather than being sealed up tight, has open borders. We humans evolved relationally; we exist interdependently;

our very existence depends on interaction with the rest of the natural world. This broader context provides the condition today to rethink the scope and significance of the incarnation in an ecological direction. The flesh that the Word became is part of the vast body of the cosmos.

Deep incarnation

The phrase "deep incarnation" is starting to be used in theology as a kind of shorthand to signify that the incarnation implies a radical divine reach through human flesh in Jesus Christ into the very matrix of biological existence itself with its growth and decay. From the beginning, God had the character of being a friend of the material world, creating it, sustaining it, calling it good, blessing it, receiving its praise. Incarnation effects a new level of union. Let us consider this insight in the words of Danish theologian Niels Gregersen, who coined the phrase deep incarnation:

> In Christ, God enters into the biological tissue of creation in order to share the fate of biological existence. In the incarnate One, God shares the life conditions of foxes and sparrows, grass and trees, soil and moisture.

Born of a woman, the Word of God became a creature of earth, a complex unit of minerals and fluids, an item in the carbon, oxygen, and nitrogen cycles, a moment in the biological evolution of this planet. The genes of the cells in his body were kin to the flowers, frogs, fish, finches, foxes, the whole community of life that descended from common ancestors in the ancient seas. Deep incarnation understands John 1:14 to be saying that the flesh which the Word of God became not only connects Jesus Christ to other human beings. It also reaches beyond them to join him to the whole biological world of living creatures and the cosmic dust of which they are composed.

Viewing Jesus as Emmanuel or God-with-us in this way entails a belief not at all obvious for monotheistic faith in one God which Christians share with Jewish and Muslim traditions. While still maintaining unquestioned belief in one God, incarnation affirms the radical notion that in Jesus Christ the one transcendent God who creates and empowers the world freely chooses to join this world in the flesh. As a result, a certain bold logic takes hold: if this is God, then thus is God. Jesus's life now forms an essential part of the story that Christians tell about God. The one Creator relates to the world not as a dictator who dominates but as a humble, compassionate and serving lover.

A densely specific expression of the love of God already poured out in creation, incarnation confers a new form of nearness to God on the whole of earthly reality in its bodily dimensions, on all of Earth's creatures, on the plants, animals, and ecosystems, and on the cosmos in which our planet dynamically exists. God's own self-expressive Word personally joins the biological world as a member of the human race, and via this perch on the tree of life enters into solidarity with the whole bio-physical cosmos of which human beings are a part. This deep incarnation of God within the biotic community of life forges a new kind of union. While the Spirit of God, the Giver of life, is present everywhere throughout the created world, the incarnation bespeaks a different form of divine presence, one marked by an unimaginable intimacy. It is presence in the flesh.

Bodies Matter

For someone later interpreted mainly as a spiritual Savior, it is remarkable how strongly Jesus's characteristic teaching and deeds focused on bodies. His healing practices placed people's bodily suffering at the center of concern. He used the touch of his warm hand and his own spittle mixed with earth (the mud pie ritual!) to convey health. And how he fed people! Large numbers on hillsides and in smaller groups around home tables knew firsthand his desire to nourish hungry bodies as well as thirsting spirits. The surrounding natural world provided examples for his parables, and he looked upon plants and animals with a loving gaze. The dualism of later Christian thought that drove a wedge between body and spirit simply did not occur to him. The God of his heart was the Creator of heaven and earth, and everything was encompassed in the good news he announced.

Contemplating Jesus Christ through the lens of deep incarnation, we come to see the world with new eyes. We begin to grasp what Sallie McFague colorfully describes as the christic paradigm. This is a pattern gleaned from the life, death, and resurrection of Jesus which clarifies that "liberating, healing, and inclusive love is the meaning of it all." Love as Jesus enfleshed it reveals the ineffable compassion of God. This love is the meaning encoded at the core of human life and at the heart of the universe itself. Plenitude of life for all, not just for one species or for an elite group in that species but for all, including poor human beings and all living creatures, is God's original and ultimate intent. It is not only souls that are important. Physical bodies, gifted with dignity, also matter to God: all bodies, not only those beautiful and full of life but also those damaged, violated, starving, dying, bodies of humankind and otherkind alike.

Let us ponder this mystery of faith, that the Word was made flesh. Let it lead to the realization that the historical arc of Jesus's life reveals God's compassion for all the bodies in creation.

I am the bountiful Lord, the God of all flesh.

—Jeremiah 32:27

17

The cross and the tree of life

At three o'clock Jesus cried out with a loud voice, "Eloi, Eloi, lama sabachthani?" which means, "My God, my God, why have you forsaken me?"

—Mark 15:34

Meditating on God and the earth in view of Jesus's tormented death on the cross must needs start with a moment of stunned silence. The Catholic ritual on Good Friday gets it exactly right. It begins with utter quiet as the presider simply enters and lies face down on the floor, prostrate before the altar. A deep hush settles over the congregation. There are no words.

Crucifixion. Jesus's life ended in a tortured death of the worst sort. He was dragged through physical breakdown and godforsakenness into the darkness of the tomb. True, there he was met not by annihilation but by the creative power of the Giver of life who transformed his defeat into unimaginable new life. But his death was real. Let us not skip over his brutal end too quickly.

It is crucial to remember that the main Christian symbol is not a deathbed but a cross. Jesus did not die a natural death as a result of sickness, old age, or being eaten by a lion. His life was violently ripped from him by crucifixion, a deliberate political act. This was an agonizing method of execution carried out by the state and reserved for slaves and others who were not Roman citizens. It was meant as an example to instill terror into conquered peoples: obey the Empire or you too will end up like this.

In Jesus's case, his death was the result of wrongful human decisions by political authorities. They could have decided differently. Instead, the power of empire rolled on at full throttle and this prophet from Galilee paid an excruciating price for fidelity to his ministry. His life ended terribly, bleeding out in a spasm of unjust state violence. While some women disciples kept vigil by the cross—it was the women who stayed—other followers ran and hid. His ministry came crashing down. The joy of teaching, healing, feasting, all came to a violent halt. He was overcome with a feeling of being abandoned even by the gracious and merciful God whose coming reign he had preached. This was a horrific death, raked with physical, psychological, and spiritual suffering.

The character of God

That the human being Jesus suffered an agonizing death on the cross is a given of history. That in this event it was the Word of God made flesh who suffered and died is an affirmation of faith, a claim made on the basis of the incarnation: if this is God, thus is God. Here we have an astonishing new chapter of God's relationship to creation, namely, "I am with you" in the flesh even unto a suffering death. Having tasted the dregs of rejection and physical agony, the crucified Christ knows what it means to suffer. In his own body, he knows. This knowing is embedded in the very heart of the living God.

Consider how the Greek word *kenosis*, self-emptying, expresses the character of God revealed in the cross. In a letter to the church in Philippi, Paul encourages members of the community to be of the same mind as Christ Jesus, who though he was in the form of God did not regard equality with God something to be clung to, "but emptied himself," taking the form of a slave, being born human, and becoming obedient, even to death on a cross (Phil 2:7). This tremendous swoop from divine form to crucified human form traces an arc of divine humility. It credits the ineffable God with having a non-godly characteristic, especially when seen against the traditional model of God as an omnipotent monarch, namely, the ability to be self-limiting, self-offering, vulnerable, self-giving, in a word, creative Love in action. The shocking contrast to what we expect divinity to be reveals the unfathomable depths of God's unconditional love. Far from stripping omnipotence away, divine participation in suffering expresses the kind of power God actually exercises. It takes omnipotence to be able to love like this.

For all who die

The implications for those who suffer and die, both humans and others, are profound.

For Christians everywhere across the centuries, Jesus Christ's solidarity with each person who dies brings the presence of God into this bleakest of moments. He tasted death for everyone, as the letter to the Hebrews put it (2:9). The pain, the darkness of dying, even godforsakenness, do not separate persons from God who creates and loves them. Clinging to this faith, some may take comfort. For all there is hope.

The crucified people

One of the gifts of the Black church in the United States to the whole church is the conviction that Jesus's brutal death by crucifixion reveals in a particular way God's solidarity with victims of injustice. The music of the spirituals, produced during centuries of enslavement, brings this to poignant expression. In these songs, as African American theologian M. Shawn Copeland explains, people sang of the cross not because they were masochistic and enjoyed suffering. Rather,

> the enslaved Africans sang because they saw on the rugged wooden planks the One who had endured what was their daily portion. The cross was treasured because it enthroned the One who went all the way with them and for them. The enslaved Africans sang because they saw the results of the cross—triumph over the principalities and powers of death, triumph over evil in this world.

Making a stunning comparison between Jesus hung on a wooden cross and the strange fruit of lynched Black people hung from trees in the Jim Crow era, James Cone elaborates:

> black Christians believed that just knowing Jesus went through an experience of suffering in a manner similar to theirs gave them faith that God was with them, even in suffering on lynching trees, just as God was present with Jesus in suffering on the cross.

Here the cross is a symbol of resistance. The final word about Black life is not death on a lynching tree but redemption in the cross, "a miraculously transformed life found in the God of the gallows."

Latin American liberation theology, arising from communities of people struggling against grinding poverty, violence, and political lack of voice, names a similar awful reality: crosses keep on being set up in history. It is not just individuals who hang there, but whole social groups. These are those whom Ignacio Ellacuría, the Salvadoran martyr, called the "crucified people." Their suffering is not natural but due to the way society is organized and run for the benefit of a privileged few. Christ identifies with these people who are so crucified: "As long as you did it to one of the least of these brothers and sisters of mine, you did it to me" (Matt 25:40). Just as God was present with Hebrew people enslaved in Egypt, and with the wrongly accused and unjustly executed Jesus of Nazareth, so too the redeeming God sees, hears, and knows well what oppressed peoples are suffering and is present with the intent to save. "Go, I am sending you to Pharaoh": the divine mission rolls through the centuries from Moses at the burning bush to the church today. Impelled by the Spirit, followers of Jesus are called to go and make every effort to take the crucified people down from the cross through awakening consciousness, communal resistance to wrongs, and action on behalf of justice for social transformation.

The crucified species

There is yet further meaning in the unfathomably awful event of the cross.

The sheer fact that Jesus died means that he shared the fate of all who die, which is every living thing. While theology has traditionally emphasized Jesus's solidarity with human beings who die, whether naturally or as a result of sinful violence, he was related in the flesh to all the branches of the evolutionary tree of life. The logic of deep incarnation gives a strong warrant for extending the solidarity of the cross into the groan of suffering and the silence of death of all creatures. All creatures come to an end; those with nervous systems know pain and suffering. Jesus's anguished end places him among this company. The ineffable compassion of God revealed by the cross embraces all who are perishing, not disdaining them in their distress.

Understood in this way, Niels Gregersen declares, "the death of Christ becomes an icon of God's redemptive co-suffering with all sentient life as well as the victims of social injustice."

It is as if by inhabiting the inside of the isolating shell of death, Christ crucified brings divine life into closest contact with disaster, setting up a gleam of light for all other living beings who suffer that same annihilating suffocation. In their suffering and dying, they are not left alone. Seen through the lens of deep incarnation, Calvary graphically shows that the transcendent God of suffering love abides with all creatures, bearing the cost of new life through endless millennia of evolution, from the extinction of whole species to every sparrow that falls to the ground.

One may well ask, what difference does this make? Living creatures still suffer and die. Yes, in the nature of things, every living being dies. But the cross affirms the presence of God amid the shocking enormity of pain and death. The indwelling, empowering Creator Spirit abides amid the agony and loss. God who is love is there, in solidarity with the creatures shot through with pain and finished by death; there, in the godforsaken moment, as only the Giver of life can be, with the promise of something more.

Biologically speaking, new life continuously comes from death, over time. Theologically speaking, the cross gives grounds to hope that the presence of the crucified God in the midst of pain bears creation forward with an unimaginable promise. This does not solve the problem of suffering in a neat systematic way. It does make a supreme difference in what might come next. "We know that the whole creation has been groaning together as it suffers together the pains of labor"; but "creation itself will be set free from its enslavement to decay and will obtain the freedom of the glory of the children of God" (Rom 8:22, 21).

Care for our Common home

At this time of ecological crisis when twigs upon branches of the tree of life are rapidly going extinct, the crucified Christ's solidarity with victims extends organically to all species under threat. Their demise is not due to natural causes but to wrongful human action and inaction. As once with the Hebrew slaves, God who creates the wild, good world sees, hears, and knows their distress, and is with them. The vital Christian response, in union with all people of good will on this planet of pain, is to go and make every effort take the crucified species down from the cross through intensive action to protect and restore the natural world.

Darkness is my one companion left.
—Psalm 88:18

18
Deep resurrection: hope in God

You are the hope of all the ends of the earth,
and of the far distant seas.
—Psalm 65:5

Hope at the end

Who is this "You" whom the ends of the earth and distant seas address as their hope? What kind of God is it who holds out hope for lands and waters and their inhabitants? Obviously this is the same merciful and gracious God who creates and sustains them in being at every moment. Other psalms depict the earth and sea, filled with the juice of life, singing out praises to God with joy. But this prayer strikes a different chord. It declares hope, an attitude that normally arises in the face of limits. Grass fades, flowers wither, mountains and hills turn to dust, green plants, animals, and people die.

It is not only individuals whose time comes to an end. One day all life on planet Earth will end when the sun, reaching the end of its fuel, expands like a giant fireball and burns everything to a crisp (about five billion years from now, according to reliable calculations). Thanks to the Hubble and Webb telescopes, we can see stars themselves, once thought to be fixed points of light, being born in stellar nurseries. When they escape from their dusty crèches they blaze away for billennia, then collapse and pass on their substances to future stars and planets. Ashes to ashes, dust to dust. The universe itself will end at some point.

Does it all come to nothing? Does all the wonder and beauty, affection and comfort, struggle and becoming, pain and agony amount in the end to no more than an empty void? Perhaps. With enormous courage of spirit, biblical faith has a different outcome in view. Thanks to the living God who is ever-faithful, the world can hope for something more that lies ahead, a renewal of all creation. To be honest, we cannot begin to imagine this. But "in accord with God's promise we await new heavens and a new earth, where justice dwells" (2 Pet 3:13).

Christ's resurrection

In the Christian tradition, this hope pivots on the death and resurrection of Jesus Christ. The Easter narratives witness that the crucified Jesus died not into nothingness but into the loving embrace of the mystery of God who enfolded him with affection in new transfigured life. Joyful Alleluias ring out at Easter because we realize this blessed destiny is not meant for Jesus alone. Given his solidarity with the human race, we hope that the future for human beings will be on a broad scale what has already happened for him. The early hymn which sings that Christ is "the firstborn from the dead" (Col 1:18) is making the point that others will follow; the firstborn is not the only born. Christians trust that "the power of God who raised him from the dead" (Col 2:12) will be with the rest of us human beings also in our suffering and dying and speak a new word of life over our completed lives.

Is this blessed future meant for only one species? Or does it encompass the whole of creation in its awesome variety? In view of Jesus's solidarity in the flesh with all creatures who live and die, faith in God rolls the story forward and holds deep resurrection hope not only for human beings but for the whole natural world. A blessed future will dawn for the whole community of creation and every one of its creatures. Karl Rahner penned dramatic words spelling out the universality at stake: "His resurrection is like the first eruption of a volcano which shows that in the interior of the world God's fire is already burning, and this will bring everything to blessed ardor in its light. He has risen to show that this has already begun."

The claim has a clear logic. It sets out from the insight that Jesus of Nazareth was a genuine part of the historical and biological community of life on Earth. Made of star stuff and earth stuff, his body existed in a network of relationships drawn from the whole physical universe. As a child of Earth he died, and the earth claimed him back in a grave. Raised from the dead, he has been reborn not as a pure spirit but as a member of the earth community, radiantly transfigured. One with the flesh of the earth, his risen humanity bears the hope that the future transformation of the world will be the final salvation of everything, including the groaning community of life, brought into a blessed future by the holy God of love. This vision sings out in the same early hymn which called Christ the firstborn from the dead. While this might be taken to mean only the human dead, the hymn also names him "the firstborn of all creation" (Col 1:15). With good reason the fourth-century bishop Ambrose of Milan could preach, "In Christ's resurrection the earth itself arose."

The Intelligence of Hope

Lest this be dismissed as a fantasy, it is important to be clear about what is being claimed. There is a tendency in some quarters today to shy away from the idea of resurrection as if it were wishful thinking, a kind of magical belief based on pious legends, a sensational oddity that faith in a secular age might well do without. It seems escapist, a fanciful way to blunt the harsh reality of death. Some artistic renderings of the risen Christ may contribute to this unease.

To the contrary, resurrection must be understood with the intelligence of hope. Consider two basic points that interpret resurrection within the frame of today's sensibility.

Promised but unknown

First, resurrection in the concrete is not seriously imaginable to us who still live within the time-space grid of our universe. It is beyond the horizon of what anyone can literally know. We do have glimpses or foretastes here and there of a magnificent fullness of life when justice is done, beauty appears, love becomes visible in joy, liberation and healing. But death itself is an impenetrable frontier, "the undiscovered country from whose bourn no traveler returns" (Shakespeare, *Hamlet* 3.1). Using empirical methods we cannot prove that anything lies beyond death; neither can we prove that nothing lies beyond. Those who die enter into a great silence. No one comes back from the dead to render a report, as imagined in the resuscitation of a corpse. The finitude of human knowing needs to be respected.

Biblical scholarship today points out that the gospel stories of Jesus's resurrection proceed with respect for this point. The resurrection of the crucified was not an observable, public event. No one saw it happen. None of the gospels describe it as an event in historical terms. There is an empty tomb. Mary Magdalene and the other myrrh-bearing women who discover this emptiness encounter Jesus in visionary religious experiences, as do other disciples. To describe the indescribable, the New Testament rightly uses pictorial language such as Jesus being raised up, awakening from sleep, being alive again. But these are pointers to a transcendent event of great goodness that lies beyond imagination. In

Paul's inimitable words, "no eye has seen, nor ear heard, nor the human heart conceived" what lies in store, but these things "God has revealed to us through the Spirit" (1 Cor 2:9–10).

The appearances of the risen Christ are a revelation, grasped and appreciated only with the eyes of faith. This point clears the deck of unwarranted literalism.

Radical belief in God

The second point fills this unimaginable, empty space with the action of the living God who, it must be remembered, is not a being among other beings, not even a Supreme Being, but the inconceivable holy mystery of Love who creates, sustains, and will complete the world. Resurrection dares to assert that this ineffable Love was with Jesus in the darkness of his dying in such a way that, having crossed that frontier, Jesus emerges quickened into a new kind of life. "Why do you look for the living among the dead? He is not here, but has risen" (Luke 24:5); "He is not here; for he has been raised" (Matt 28:6).

Resurrection refers to a creative act of God that transforms the whole historical person of Jesus into new life in glory through the power of the Spirit, thereby releasing his presence throughout the world. This is not simply belief in the immortality of the soul. It does not envision Jesus shucking off his humanity like a suit of clothes and rising heavenward into pure divinity. Rather, his entire human historical reality in all its undivided dimensions is pervaded by the vivifying Spirit of God and made whole in a new way. The crucified one lives forever in the ineffable life of the creative God who completes everything in love.

Far from being an esoteric fantasy, then, resurrection hope is actually a *consequence* of belief in God who creates heaven and earth. Ponder this for a minute. Do not fall into the trap of divorcing God who creates from God who redeems. The one God who creates the world also blazes forth from the burning bush as One who sees the misery of slaves, hears their cries, knows their sufferings, and comes to deliver them (Exod 3:7–8). This same God rests upon Jesus and anoints him to proclaim good news to the poor, release to captives, recovery of sight to the blind, and freedom to the oppressed (Luke 4:18). In the light of Jesus's death and resurrection, this same God is defined in one amazing word as "love" (1 John 4:8). This is the same Creator who made heaven and earth and all that is in them, and who has intimate knowledge of the solstices and changing seasons, the tempers of wild animals, the varieties of plants and the virtues of roots (Wis 7:17–22).

Since the loving Creator can call the creature from not-being into being, then this same Creator, acting with the same infinite power of love, can also call the creature from death to life. This is what resurrection is all about. Swiss theologian Hans Küng made the point in stunning words: "Belief in the resurrection is not an appendage to belief in God; it is precisely the radicalization of belief in God." It is belief in God that does not stop halfway but follows the road consistently to the end, trusting that the Alpha who had the first word over our lives is also the Omega who will have the last word, and it is the same loving word: "Let there be life."

To believe in the resurrection is not to believe in a scientific miracle. It is to believe in God. It is an act of hope in the God who created you and everyone else and everything else, who has the love and the power still to recreate, even when death has taken away the only life that you know. Not wishful thinking, then, or an unverifiable curiosity, resurrection hope is rooted in belief in God, in God's fidelity to creation.

Creation, again

The connection between creation and resurrection appears in several insightful biblical texts. During a persecution against the

Jews, the mother of seven sons who were being executed for their fidelity to covenant law used her own experience of pregnancy to encourage the youngest:

> I do not know how you came into being in my womb. It was not I who gave you life and breath, nor I who set in order the elements within each of you. Therefore the Creator of the world, who shaped the beginning of humankind and devised the origin of all things, will in his mercy give life and breath back to you again, since you now forget yourselves for the sake of his laws. (2 Macc 7:22–23).

Note how she reasons, from wonder at the marvel of each of her new babies to the conviction that God who creates them, along with the whole world, is surely able to give life once again, even after death. Her faith in God is radical, down to the root, all the way to the end.

The apostle Paul made the same connection between creation and resurrection. Writing about God in whom Abraham believed, he says succinctly that this is the God "who gives life to the dead and calls into being the things that do not exist" (Rom 4:17). The parallel in these two divine actions is telling. There is nothing; the Creator calls forth a world. There is death, again nothing; this same gracious and merciful God calls forth new life. Creation and resurrection are tightly interwoven. No creature remains outside the dominion of the One who is Creator and endlessly treasures all that has been made.

To hope for resurrection, then, is not to cling to a strange phenomenon but to believe in God who creates the world, the living God who raised Jesus from the dead. In death and from death Jesus experienced "a homecoming into God's mystery." He passed beyond the dimension of our space and our time into the incomprehensibly loving domain of the fecund Source of all, whom people call God. His resurrection, a blessed consummation of his whole person, occurs as a divine pledge for the future of the whole world. With the new creation of resurrection as with original and ongoing creation, everything depends on the character of God.

A FUTURE FOR ALL

"You are the hope of all the ends of the earth, and of the far distant seas" (Ps 65:5). In praying this way the psalm makes room for the whole evolving natural world to be included in the central proclamation of Christian salvation. Impossible to imagine, this blessed future is poorly served by efforts to picture details, by questions such as will the dinosaurs be there or how will we all fit. It is beyond our capacity to know in the concrete. What is within reach is hope, a response to the graced call to trust, to have confidence that the Creator will not abandon the beloved creation, and to bank on that fidelity in the face of dissolution and death.

Looking from the cross and resurrection of Jesus, we can now see an infinitely compassionate divine presence accompanying Earth and all its creatures in their living and striving, suffering and dying. Since God who creates and empowers the evolutionary world also joins the fray in Jesus Christ, personally drinking the cup of suffering and going down into death, affliction even at its worst does not have the last word. The evolving world of life, all of matter in its endless permutations, will not be left behind but will be transfigured by the resurrecting action of the Creator God. The land, seas, and every creature will be blessed according to their own nature as part of the whole creation that will be made new.

EASTER HOPE

The great liturgical ritual of the Easter Vigil uses beautiful symbols that evoke this ecological realization. In a dark church or under a dark sky, a great candle is lit from newly-struck fire. Its flame, marvelously undimmed, spreads from small candle to small candle held by participants and lights up the darkness. An exulting hymn calls upon the whole earth to rejoice because Christ is risen, twice acknowledging the bees whose labors made the candle wax. The first reading is the story of creation from the book of Genesis, followed by other biblical texts that highlight the story of salvation. Generous use of flowers and greens, water for baptism, oil for anointing, and bread and wine for eucharistic sharing all express the cosmic reach of the Morning Star who never sets, Christ risen from the dead, whose peaceful light illumines the earth and all its creatures.

Amid a fractured world, awash in violence, struggling against injustice, dark with daily death, every Easter is a celebration of the whole of creation promised transformation by the presence of the risen Christ. In life he was part of the community of creation; in death he is in solidarity with all who die; in new life he anchors hope for the whole world. Although we humans have been inclined to separate our species from the others and reserve heaven for our distinguished though sinning selves alone, the earth and its inhabitants are created by the same generous God and share in the identity of being beloved creatures. For all our human difference, this shared identity makes us kin with the land, sea, and sky, and with the horse, the salmon, the crow, the ant, the olive tree, and the estuary in one grand community of creation destined for joy.

> *Creation itself will be set free from its enslavement to decay and will obtain the freedom of the glory of the children of God.*
>
> —Romans 8:21

19
Salvation even for elephants?

You save humans and animals alike, O gracious Lord.
—Psalm 36:6

Years ago while teaching in South Africa, I gave a public lecture presenting the biblical belief that all creation would be redeemed. Having recently visited that country's Kruger National Park and been awed by seeing Africa's marvelous animals roaming in the wild, I was moved to depart from my prepared text to say that lions, hippos, giraffes, impala, wildebeest, storks, termites, the whole lot, had a blessed future in store. The local Catholic newspaper disagreed. It ran an article critical of my talk under the headline "Salvation Even for Elephants?" It is a great springboard question.

A lost belief

If you asked almost anyone brought up in the Western Christian tradition, they would most likely say this teaching about all of creation being redeemed is a mistake. Unlike the Eastern Orthodox tradition, Western theology has taught that while animals are indeed created by God, they do not have a future. Hence they disappear from prayer and thought when the focus shifts to salvation. This erasure is due not only to the strongly-held idea that animals rank lower than human beings in the hierarchy of being, have no intrinsic value, and therefore are not included in God's redeeming plan. It also results from starting the theology of salvation with human sin. Whether explicitly or implicitly, the Genesis story of Adam and Eve's disobedience colors the background in Western discussion of salvation. All human beings have sinned. The good news is that God graciously offers us redemption through the life, death, and resurrection of Jesus Christ. Such a focus on sin ensures that the destiny of only human beings is at stake when the question of salvation is raised.

It is certainly true that human beings sin in horrific ways and need God's mercy. But limiting salvation to one species alone shortchanges the richness of biblical teaching about God's desire to save. It is also woefully inadequate in light of the devastating climate emergency gripping our planet. Wrecked ecosystems and the extinction of thousands of plant and animal species along with misery for human communities, especially those afflicted because of climate change, cry out for a more inclusive understanding of salvation.

A first step toward including animals in the community of the redeemed entails widening the meaning of salvation. As part of the evolving world, animals come into being and pass away. They need to be saved, delivered, snatched not from the snare of sin, like humans, but from suffering and death. The very meaning of the biblical word "salvation" shares a common root with the word for healing. A medical practitioner brings people safely through an illness and restores them to health; he or she saves their life. Over time, "to save" expanded beyond physical healing to encompass other kinds of rescue, coming to mean deliverance from all kinds of harm. When used in a religious context, salvation expands even further to mean the ultimate healing of life's wounds and fractures in the gift of new life thanks to the gracious goodness of God.

Inclusive salvation

As part of a litany of divine characteristics, Psalm 36 makes a rarely noticed claim:

> Your steadfast love reaches to the heavens,
> your faithfulness to the clouds.
> Your righteousness is like the mighty mountains,
> your judgments are like the great deep;
> you save humans and animals alike, O gracious
> Lord. (Ps 36:5–6)

Parsing this text which is rarely discussed, biblical scholar Ken Stone observes that the verb translated as "save," *yasha*, is not a minor word in the Hebrew Bible. It is a common verbal root used in many different texts to speak about divine acts of salvation, deliverance and liberation, and in multiple references to God as Savior. Stone's analysis leads to a keen insight: "By making animals as well as humans the objects of God's salvation, and using such vocabulary to do so, Psalm 36 places animals firmly within the redemptive activity of God that is often understood as central to biblical religion."

In response, animals look hopefully to God and wait for divine goodness (Ps 145:15), activities ascribed elsewhere to human speakers who look to God and wait in hope for salvation (see Ps 123:2 and Ps 27:14). Encompassed in the circle of salvation, animals rely on their Maker whose loving-kindness cares about their lives.

Inheriting this conviction, the New Testament simply presupposes that animals are included in salvation, which is cosmic in scope. Occasionally this surfaces in specific ways, such as the risen Christ's mandate to the disciples to "Go into the whole world and proclaim the gospel to every creature" (Mark 16:15), the gospel being the good news of salvation. The inclusive vision shows up again in an epistle writer's encouragement to hold firm to "the hope promised by the gospel that you heard, which has been proclaimed to every creature under heaven" (Col 1:23). Ordinarily, animals are just part of the larger picture of a redeemed world. Notice that when Paul makes the hopeful assertion that "creation itself will be set free from its bondage to decay and will obtain the freedom of the glory of the children of God" (Rom 8:21), there are no exceptions.

God who loves the earth

In the lead-up to Psalm 36's affirmation that the living God saves humans and animals alike, the prayer enlists distant points of geography to describe the kind of Creator who would act this way:

- One who loves with an affection as steadfast as the sky is high.
- Blessed mystery who is faithful with a tenacity that reaches to the clouds.
- Spirit who is righteous with a love of justice as enduring as magnificent mountains.
- Giver of life who judges wisely with insight deeper than the depths of the ocean.

These wondrous natural phenomena—the sky and its weather, the land and its massive formations, the sea and its unfathomable depths—all give some faint sense of the character of the Creator

Spirit who made them. Mirrored in the planet's marvels, their Creator is loving, steadfastly faithful, a partisan for justice, and wise beyond all telling. With such a God, the promise of wide-ranging salvation inclusive of animals is a much more reasonable hope than is the alternative, that they would be forgotten and annihilated.

An intriguing story about the nineteenth-century naturalist John Muir brings this biblical hope into the venue of the American west. One day when Muir was hiking in the Yosemite wilderness he came upon a dead bear. He stopped to reflect on this creature's dignity. Here was an animal with warm blood and a heart that pumped like ours, one who rejoiced to feel the warm sun on his fur, and for whom a good day was finding a bush filled with berries. Later Muir wrote a bitter entry in his journal criticizing the religious folk he knew who made no room in their faith for such noble creatures. They think they are the only ones with souls, he complained, the only ones for whom heaven is reserved. To the contrary, he wrote, "God's charity is broad enough for bears."

Let us ponder these generous words. The claim is the result of Muir's intense admiration for an animal, to be sure, but its roots are religious. Is God's charity broad enough for bears? What would you say? Are black bears, panda bears, polar bears, grizzly bears the recipients of divine love to the extent that in their suffering and death they are affected by God's redeeming power? Does God save humans and animals alike?

Each creature, resplendently transfigured

Pope Francis would say yes. All through *Laudato Si'* he emphasizes that our planet is God's good creation, that all beings form one community of creation, and that humans are responsible for caring for our common home. Carrying this insight through to the end, the letter's conclusion paints a daring picture of heaven. Unlike the writer of Psalm 36, the pope writes with urgency due to contemporary devastation of planet Earth as a dwelling place for life. But his understanding of the broadness of God's mercy resonates consistently with Muir's insight as well as that of the psalm. "At the end, we will find ourselves face to face with the infinite beauty of God," Francis writes, describing heaven which, of course, is indescribable. Enfolded with affection, we humans will not find ourselves alone, for also present will be the whole universe, "which with us will share in unending plenitude." Lest we pass over this point without registering its import, the next sentence makes it explicit. "Eternal life will be a shared experience of awe, in which each creature, resplendently transfigured, will take its rightful place and have something to give those poor men and women who will have been liberated once and for all" (*LS* 243).

Each creature, resplendently transfigured! Christ is the firstborn of all creation, the firstborn of all the dead of Darwin's tree of life. Together the whole community of creation will be at home in the beauty of God, just as now, in time, our common home is the Earth.

As a deliberate religious teaching, this vision has profound ethical implications. If we can see that the whole evolving community of life is part of the redeemed future, then broad charity for bears, to say nothing of skunks, sharks, seagulls, spiders, sycamore trees, soils, indeed the whole natural world, will be part of our relationship with God and will flow into action on behalf of eco-justice as an essential part of Christian life.

Salvation even for elephants? Most assuredly yes. God is not a throw-away Creator.

> *Then I heard every creature in heaven and on earth and under the earth and in the sea and all that is in them, singing, "To the one seated on the throne and to the Lamb be blessing and honor and glory and might forever and ever!"*
>
> —Revelation 5:13

20
A world of grace

The love of God has been poured out into our hearts through the holy Spirit given to us.

—Romans 5:5

Being borne up

On the subject of creation, the usual tendency has been for thinkers to draw on philosophy's ideas of action, influence, or causality, to explain how we can think about God creating the world. That is fine in itself and does go some distance to help us understand. In light of the experience of Jesus Christ, another approach opens up. Karl Rahner, for one, has argued that if we see the created world emerging thanks to the self-giving love of God, then the "proper place for achieving an understanding of the immanent presence and creative action of God in the world . . . is not a treatise on God worked out in abstract metaphysical terms, but rather the treatise on grace." Here is an important clue. Start with the way God in Christ acts in relation to human beings and see that the Creator Spirit acts in the same way throughout the natural world. Let us see where this leads.

One difficulty at the outset is that for centuries the traditional treatise on grace objectified grace, making "it" almost into some kind of substance. Grace was some special thing that could be gained and lost and found again, as described in neo-scholastic theology. People were born without it, received it in baptism, lost it through mortal sin, gained it back through confession. Grace functioned as a kind of "third thing" between God and human beings.

Finding our way back to the basic meaning of grace in scripture, however, we see it is a way of speaking about the loving presence of God who is "gracious." The word refers to divine favor, divine affection, a vast and lavish self-giving love. Rahner picked this up and described grace as God's self-communication, God's own self-giving love bestowed on human beings. Rather than something other than God, to paraphrase Rahner, with the gift of grace the Giver's own self is the gift. This gift is bestowed freely and generously on all people without being earned or merited. We may reject the gift of divine love but the offer is never withdrawn, because God is faithful. The effect is to heal, to forgive, to comfort, to challenge, to enlighten, to inspire, to draw us closer, as needed, while ever respectful of human freedom. Some have compared the experience of grace to being lovingly held by another, not that we grasp God but that God holds onto us and smiles on us as a loving parent on a precious child.

The experience of grace can be amazing, as the famous hymn sings. It invites the gift of our own selves in response. This may take the form of dramatic conversion from a loveless path in our life harmful to others, as was the case with the wretched slave-trader John Newton who wrote "Amazing Grace." He once was lost but now is found, was blind but now he sees. Grace brings healing to sinful hearts and justice to broken situations. Again, without drama, the experience of grace may quietly attract us to what is good, strengthen our fidelity on ordinary days, and sustain us in desolation. Over a lifetime grace moves us to deepen our love of God and to grow in a love of neighbor that acts for their well-being, even at cost to ourselves.

The poet Denise Levertov expressed the experience of grace in memorable images of floating and flying:

As swimmers dare
to lie face to the sky
and water bears them,
as hawks rest upon air
and air sustains them,
so would I learn to attain
freefall, and float
into Creator Spirit's deep embrace,
knowing no effort earns
that all-surrounding grace.

One constant of the experience, attested by anyone who speaks of it, is that grace attracts but never forces. The love of God calls. The compassion of God invites response. But humans are free to reject the offer. They can and do sin. Nevertheless, the offer persists. This is how human beings experience interaction with divine mercy.

Roll this over to God's creative activity in the evolving natural world. There is no forcing. With human beings, God's Spirit graciously prods, pushes, pulls, lures the heart in loving relationship, but the freedom of the creature remains. As with humans, so too with all of creation. Rather than being a rarity, God's gracious love that powerfully invites but never coerces is typical of the divine way of acting in the natural world. The evolving world, functioning without compulsion according to its own inner dynamics, responds freely to the gracious call of the ever-present Creator Spirit to come on ahead.

Christ is the key

In Christian experience, the life, death, and resurrection of Jesus Christ make the pattern of this gracious love especially clear. The gospels portray Jesus's vigorous teaching and dealings with people as being very attractive to some while off-putting and even dangerous to others. The invitation to follow him was loud and clear, but no one was ever coerced. Toward the end of John's gospel, written in the light of the resurrection, the author notes that Jesus did many more things than could be recorded in this book, but these things were written so you could believe and "through believing you may have life in his name" (20:31). In accord with the spirit of Jesus, the gospel's approach seeks to persuade and convince, inviting readers to come and see for themselves. But no one is compelled to believe.

"Christ is the key to how the Spirit works," in Kathryn Tanner's felicitous phrase. For all Christian theology, the gospel is good news. The love of God made known through Christ is a saving, healing, restoring power that benefits human beings. When this becomes the starting point for thinking about creation, then a lovely logic takes over. We have a warrant for thinking that as with humans, so too with the natural world within which we have evolved. Perceived through the Christ event, the gracious God, Spirit proceeding as love in person, is present to bless and empower the world's natural processes rather than to override them.

The living God is trustworthy and acts consistently. All creation is treated in ways similar to God's gracious ways with human beings. Take a moment to reflect on the experience of grace in your own life. Ponder Christ's own active presence through thick and thin. Let it illuminate how the living God acts in the wider context of the natural world.

From Christ's fullness we have all received, grace upon grace.

—John 1:16

Humankind and Otherkind

21

Dominion? Genesis 1 or Job

When I look at your heavens, the work of your fingers,
the moon and the stars that you have made;
what is humankind that you are mindful of them,
human beings that you care for them?

—Psalm 8:3–4

If one looks at human beings through an ecological lens, we are obviously part of the network of living beings on earth, breathing the air, drinking the water, eating other creatures, being born from a mother and dying back into dust. The same connection remains clear when one looks at human beings through the lens of creation theology. Along with the moon and the stars, we are the work of God's hands, an intrinsic part of the community of creation, kin with all the rest. Given this fundamental connection, the question arises as to how human beings with our unique gifts and talents should relate with other living beings, how we should treat them. What is our proper role as fellow creatures?

Have dominion

The opening chapter of the Bible contains a verse that many people today accuse of contributing to the problem of human arrogance over other living beings (not that we need much encouragement). On the sixth day of creation, after making the domestic and wild animals that walk and slither on the land, God made yet another land animal:

> And God said "Let us make humans in our image, according to our likeness, and let them have dominion over the fish of the sea and over the birds of the air and over the cattle and over all the wild animals of the earth and over every creeping thing that creeps upon the earth."
> (Gen 1:26)

Let them have dominion. Whatever does this mean?

Let it be said loud and clear: dominion does not even remotely mean domination or permission to exploit. Let us put this vexing phrase in the context of its own Genesis chapter. The six days of creation have brought forth a vast array of creatures "of every kind" whom God delights in and pronounces "good." The earth receives a call to bring forth vegetation. The waters are invited to bring forth swarms of sea creatures. Birds and fish are given their own vocational mandate to increase and multiply. As one created being among others, humans share their own creation on the sixth day with cattle, snakes, and wild animals of every kind. And the story does not end with them. The climax of the creation narrative comes on day seven when God rests from all this work, thus making the sabbath a blessed day of rest for humans and animals alike.

In the flow of this narrative, "let them have dominion" bespeaks a profound vote of confidence in humans, male and female alike. Having created them in the divine image and likeness, God entrusts them with a god-like responsibility: "Have dominion, take good care of the others, treat them as I would, since you are made in my image and likeness and you represent me."

This is a divine call to a vocation of service, to make sure the earth flourishes. Note that no one particular type of human being is singled out. The inestimable dignity of being created in the divine image and likeness is true of every human being regardless of race, ethnicity, nationality, gender, age, economic status, sexual orientation, health, education, talent, disability, or any other marker by which we classify ourselves. It is to the whole collective group that the charge to have dominion is given.

In the biblical context, dominion often refers to a role of good governance. If a kingdom was too vast for the king himself to get around, he would send representatives to see that good order was maintained according to his will. These stand-ins for the king were understood to have dominion. The Genesis 1 framework clearly indicates that human beings, made in God's image and likeness, are called to represent the Creator who made and blessed the other species. If they live up to their God-given responsibility, others will flourish as God desires.

Today this role is more often referred to as wise stewardship. A steward manages goods that belong to someone else and is responsible to that owner for those goods remaining in decent shape or even becoming more plentiful. Having dominion means that humans are called to a responsible service of protection and care. In this role they are accountable to the owner of the other creatures, the one who says they are "mine," the Creator.

Imagine what our attitude would be like if the Bible started with Psalm 104 instead of with Genesis 1. We would start out with a deep sense of connection with others whom God makes and cares for, rather than the idea that we are dominant over all. Yes, we can read the dominion text in Genesis 1 as calling human beings to act responsibly for the rest of creation, and it is vitally important to do so. The danger, as the history of interpretation shows, is that we have a strong tendency to veer toward supremacy and rule. Without question, humans are called to responsible love and care for the earth, but this calling arises first of all from a deep belonging to the community of creation.

Where were you?

Even with the beneficent meaning of dominion in view, it comes as a surprise to discover that the role of human dominion is a minority view in scripture, appearing in Genesis 1 and Psalm 8 and seldom elsewhere. Probably because the seven-day creation story comes first in the Bible and because the story resounds with such dramatic poetic cadences, its structured view of the world with humans in charge is taken to be *the* biblical view of things. This story also receives more exposure in teaching, art, and liturgical rituals such as the Easter Vigil. But scripture itself proposes other ways of interpreting the human presence. Psalm 104 envisions human beings as kindred with others in the mix of the community of creation. There is an even more radical view scripture would have us consider.

In an extraordinary way the book of Job actually contradicts the idea that humans should have dominion over the earth, even when this role is interpreted as responsible service and care. In this story a suffering man named Job has lost everything—children, possessions, social status, bodily health. His friends say he must have sinned greatly to deserve such calamity. Convinced that this is not true, he flings protests to the heavens. In desperation he challenges God to appear in court to answer for the divine misdeed of sending so much trouble to an innocent man. In a climactic encounter God does show up. Speaking out of a whirlwind, the divine voice begins putting a series of questions to Job: "Where were you when I laid the foundation of the earth?" (Job 38:4).

Right away the mysterious Creator Spirit of the world places Job's challenge within a cosmic grandeur beyond his own ability to understand or control. The voice out of the whirlwind continues: Do you set limits to the sea? Do you make the sun come up every morning? Do you control the snow, the rain, the wind, the storms? Do you set the night tracks of constellations like the Pleiades, Orion and other stars? The questions continue:

Can you hunt prey for the lion or satisfy the appetite of the young lions?

Who provides prey for the raven when its young ones cry to God?

Do you know when the mountain goats give birth?

Who has given the wild ass its freedom?

Is the wild ox willing to serve you, to be harnessed and till your land?

Do you give the horse its terrible might or clothe its neck with a flowing mane?

Is it by your wisdom that the hawk soars and spreads its wings toward the south?

Is it by your command that the eagle mounts up and makes its nest in the rocky crag?

Can you catch the huge land animal with limbs like iron that wallows under the willows?

Can you snare the terrifying sea monster that churns the waters 'til "one would think the deep to be white-haired"? (Job 41:32).

Talk about an antidote to the idea of human dominion over the earth! With glorious poetry the text makes clear that neither the stars nor the sea, the wild animals nor the weather are subject to Job's command. And this is how it should be, in God's eyes. Job is but a creature.

It should be noted that God compliments Job for insisting that his suffering was not a punishment for sin. Job is correct on this point. But the meaning of his travail is hidden in the wider mystery of creation's magnificence. To digress from our subject for a moment, the story gives no rational answer to the agonizing problem of suffering. Job confesses his finitude; then his wealth, family, and health are restored.

Bill McKibben notes that the words from the whirlwind evoke strong contradictory responses. Before the magnificence of the cosmos, we feel humbled. Seeing the amazing workings of nature, we feel joyful. These responses may seem to be at odds, but both are crucially needed at this time of ecological distress. Taken together, "they are reinforcing, powerful—powerful enough, perhaps, to start changing some of the deep-seated behaviors that are driving our environmental destruction, our galloping poverty, our cultural despair." Humbled and delighted by the life around us, we can grow to know ourselves as members of a great community and step up to protect our kin.

What is the right role for human beings? Dominion interpreted as stewardship? Relinquishing control in view of nature's magnificence? First one and then the other, depending on circumstances? Ponder this while you situate yourself as a creature made in the image and likeness of God. Mindful of Genesis 1, exercise dominion, that is, perform one act of stewardship toward another creature, whether animal or plant. Then, mindful of Job, stand in awe before a sunrise or the stars, or the beauty of a tree or a landscape, or the ways of one wild or domestic animal. In both actions know that you are a mortal human being, called to neighborly love.

Where were you when I laid the foundations of the earth?
Tell me, if you have understanding.
Who determined its dimensions
and stretched out the surveying line?
What supports its foundations,
and who laid its cornerstone,
when the morning stars sang together
and all the angels shouted for joy?

—Job 38:4–7

22

Nature, a neighbor

For the fate of humans and the fate of animals is the same; as one dies, so dies the other. They all have the same breath.
—Ecclesiastes 3:19

When a scribe asked Jesus which commandment is the first of all, his answer combined two commandments from the Jewish Torah in this way:

> The first is, "Hear, O Israel: the Lord our God, the Lord is one. You shall love the Lord your God with all your heart and with all your soul and with all your mind and with all your strength." The second is this, "You shall love your neighbor as yourself." There is no other commandment greater than these. (Mark 12: 29–31)

Love God, love your neighbor. In Jesus's view the two are profoundly interrelated, the second flowing from the first, the first coming to expression in the second. For how can you love God whom you do not see if you do not love your neighbor, whom God created and endlessly treasures, whom you can see?

This teaching is core to Christian life. Over centuries it has inspired people to small and magnificent acts of goodness. In charity, give of your time and treasure to meet the needs of others: feed the hungry, visit the sick, comfort the sorrowful. In justice, organize with others to transform structures that oppress people: stand against racism, act in solidarity with those who are economically poor, who are migrating, who are trafficked.

Can nature be our neighbor too? Should we look beyond our own species to recognize "neighbor" in other living beings and in the natural world as a whole? Our biological relatedness with all other species interacting on this one planet gives this question a positive answer. So too does a robust sense of the creation relationship which sees all creatures as brothers and sisters continuously sung into being by the one Creator Spirit. A second creation story in Genesis adds a biblical warrant for seeing other creatures in this neighborly way.

The Earth Creature in the Garden

Strange as it may seem, after the first chapter of Genesis portrays God creating the world and resting on the seventh day, a second account of creation starts the process all over again. The story in Genesis chapter two is less organized than the first and has more of the coloring of a folk tale; scholars say it is much older. Instead of majestically speaking the world into being day by day (let there be, and so it was), the Creator gets down and dirty in the mud, shaping the human form from the material of the ground and then performing a kind of CPR, breathing air into the inert form. Let us dwell on two details.

First, the components. "Then the Lord God formed man from the dust of the ground and breathed into his nostrils the breath of life, and the man became a living being" (Gen 2:7). In Hebrew the word for ground (***adamah***) and the word for human being (*adam*) are closely related cognates. *Adam* is made from the *adamah*. In a very interesting alternative translation, feminist scholar Phyllis Trible proposes that *adam*, usually translated man, is not yet sexually defined. This happens in the story only when woman is created, which leads to the differentiation between male and female later in the story. Thus *adam* can rightly be translated "the earth creature" in the early part of this story. God formed the earth creature from the dust of the ground.

The importance of this word play becomes clear when other beings are created. "Out of the ground (*adamah*) the Lord God made to grow every tree that is pleasant to the sight and good for food" (Gen 2:9). And again, "Out of the ground (*adamah*) the good God formed every animal of the field and every bird of the air" (Gen 2:19). Human beings, beautiful trees that bear fruit and nuts, animals of all kinds, every flying bird, all are made from the same stuff. The dust of the ground makes beautiful bodies which are also vulnerable, subject to death across all species. This comes to expression in the Ash Wednesday ritual of marking the face with ashes with the words, "Remember that you are dust and to dust you shall return" . . . you and all other living creatures.

In similar fashion, the breath of life which God breathes into the human earth creature also vivifies other living beings. The story of the flood carries this sensibility: the animals "went into the ark with Noah, two and two of all flesh in which there was the breath of life" (Gen 7:15), as do many other texts. Human beings, beasts, birds, snakes—"everything that has the breath of life" as Genesis 1:30 puts it—all are alive thanks to the breath which is the gift of their Creator.

The reality expressed in the phrases "out of the ground" and "the breath of life" forges a link between humans, animals, and plants. From these poetic images we can glean the biblical conviction that rather than being an alien species inserted onto the planet, humans share with other creatures the same basic components of ground and breath, or body and living spirit. Talk about being kin! We have ever so much in common.

Note a second detail. Putting this deep connection into action the Creator gives the human being a nurturing, protective role. "The Lord God took the earth creature and put them in the garden of Eden to till it and keep it" (Gen 2:15). To till and keep it. Different translations of these Hebrew verbs tease out nuances of what is intended. The earth creature is given the vocation to cultivate and care for the garden; to tend and watch over it; to dress and help it; to serve and protect it. Simply put, human beings are part of the world and are meant to take care of the garden and help it flourish.

At the same time, the garden is tending to us. There is much to learn here from Indigenous Peoples. In her lovely book *Braiding Sweetgrass*, the Native American scientist Robin Wall Kimmerer describes the sensibility of her people that knows and celebrates our reciprocal relationship with the natural world. "Plants know how to make food and medicine from light and water, and then they give it away," she writes. Once we begin to listen for the languages of other beings, we can begin to understand the innumerable life-giving gifts the world provides us and learn to live with gratitude, offering our care and our own gifts in return.

Nature as Our Neighbor

Ecologically minded mystics have long addressed creatures in the natural world with terms normally reserved for other human beings. St. Francis of Assisi's "Canticle of the Creatures" shows how beautifully this can be done, as it addresses the sun, wind, air, and fire as our brother, and the moon, stars, water, and earth as our sister. Far from being a mere projection, the terms "brother" and "sister" acknowledge a real underlying relationship in the community of creation. In these meditations I have been using the term "kin" with similar meaning. "Neighbor" is another such term, heavy with biblical weight.

The modern English word "neighbor" has roots in the Old English word for "near." In ordinary usage, neighbors are those who live close by. A neighborhood is the surrounding geographic area. While local in origin, the word has a powerful ability to stretch to include people far away. Earthquake survivors need shelter and food; people who are not affected by the quake see the need via news reports and make a donation to organizations trying to provide. The word "neighbor" grows to encompass fellow human beings in need.

In a similar way, animals, plants, and microscopic organisms that live in our local area are our immediate neighbors. In a global sense, all of us living beings are neighbors made of the same stuff, connected by a long and ongoing evolutionary history, sharing the resources of the planet, interacting with every breath we take. In this ecological view, the commandment to love your neighbor extends to all the neighbors in the created world, especially those under threat. In Brian Patrick's stirring words:

> Who is our neighbor: the Samaritan? the outcast? the enemy? Yes, yes, of course. But it also the whale, the dolphin, and the rain forest. Our neighbor is the entire community of life, the entire universe. We must love it all as our self.

Loving nature as our neighbor brings strong ethical consequences. Ponder the parallel with loving the human neighbor. Acknowledging the dignity of the human person, we treat people with care and respect, paying particular attention to those most in need. Works of charity as well as actions on behalf of justice aim at shifting life away from deprivation of all kinds toward what is good. In view of the ecological crisis, Pope John Paul II declared in a striking way that the natural world should be part of this practice of love, writing: "Respect for life and for the dignity of the human person extends also to the rest of creation."

Earth's resources are bountiful but genuinely finite. Loving our neighbor means we recognize limits and share what is necessary for life with all creatures. The alternative is the reckless extinction of species and destruction of habitat that are the price of our current myopia.

Give God credit for loving the earth. Loving God with all your heart and soul, mind and strength, be converted to your own self as part of creation. Love your neighbor as yourself. Ponder how you can make the world a more compassionate place for all living beings.

> "*Which of these three, do you think, was a neighbor to the man who fell into the hands of the robbers?" The teacher of the law said, "The one who showed him mercy." Jesus said to him, "Go and do likewise."*
>
> —Luke 10:36–37

23
Pebble, peach, poodle, person

The earth is the generous Lord's with all its fullness,
the world and those that dwell therein.
—Psalm 24:1

Thinking about God as Creator who makes the world out of love brings to the fore the precious value of the natural world and the role of human beings, as members of that world, to care for its flourishing. It is regrettable that this realization has not had pride of place in Christian theology and ethics over the years. In this meditation, different from the others, we take a hard look at one of the major factors that has separated human beings from the community of creation. This factor is an ancient worldview known as the hierarchy of being. While few people today pay explicit attention to this idea, it has become woven into a common way people view themselves in relation to other species, with devastating ecological results. Taking time to ponder its shadow can equip us with the wits to walk out from under its influence.

The back story is interesting. When the early church embarked on its mission to spread the gospel, it encountered Greek philosophy, which had a strong presence in the culture around the Mediterranean Sea. In order to appeal to their hearers, Christian preachers and teachers began to use the worldview of this philosophy to interpret the gospel message. One of its key ideas held that the world was composed of two realities, spirit and matter. Spirit was more valuable because it is closer to divinity, which is pure spirit. The more "spirit" exists in a thing's composition, the closer it is to the divine. By contrast, an increase in "matter" places a thing farther away.

Using this yardstick, ancient thinkers drew up a picture of the world that ranked all beings in an arrangement called the hierarchy of being. At the lowest level and most distant from the divine are non-living things such as rocks that are simply composed of matter. Above this level come plants which grow, reproduce, and turn toward the sun, thus having a wee bit of spirit in them. Ranked even higher are animals; having more spirit they enjoy the power of locomotion. Above them at the pinnacle of life on earth are human beings with an abundance of spirit, being composed of body and soul, a powerful, rational soul with an intelligent mind and will. Higher still and closest to the divine are pure spirits who have no bodies at all, the angels.

Value ascends from the pebble to the peach to the poodle to the person to the principalities and powers, all under the rule of the Primary Cause. Such is the world structured according to the hierarchy of being. The more material a thing is, the farther away it is from God.

In our day when wealthy countries are awash in materialistic culture, when the pressure to keep on buying things affects people's daily behavior, when over-consuming has such a damaging impact on poor countries and the well-being of ecosystems and other species, there is wisdom in an ascetic approach to the use of material goods. This is a far cry, however, from disparaging matter because it is distant from God.

Note the fundamental flaw in this line of thinking. It denies the relationship of creation. It separates the living God from the physical world. But the Spirit of God dwells within the world and all its processes and creatures, sparking their existence, empowering their evolution, cherishing their every crevasse. Every rock, every leaf, every bird, every splinter of matter is sustained in being by the Spirit of God, continuously and innermostly, as fire ignites that which burns. In the reality of creation there is no possible way that matter spells out distance from God.

Theology in a hierarchical pattern

Using the dualistic matter-spirit framework, mainline Christian theology from early days onward assumed that the world was structured according to this hierarchy of being. This had a damaging impact on the value assigned to plants and animals from the perspective of faith. Aquinas, for example, argued that plants and animals, which rank lower than human beings, were created to serve human needs. Rather than being valuable in their own right, they are meant simply for human use. In technical terms, they have *instrumental* value rather than *intrinsic* value in God's eyes (note these words). Consequently, he argued, at the end of time, plants and animals will disappear. Since their purpose is to provide for our needs, once human life on earth is over, once we no longer need them for food, clothing, shelter, transportation, or working muscle, their purpose will be fulfilled. Hence they will go out of existence. No redeeming glory for them.

This hierarchical view has a strong grip on the Western Christian imagination. Thinking within its framework, theology taught that the Creator is primarily interested in human beings, the high point of creation, with humans in charge and everything else oriented to human well-being.

The hierarchy of being also turned inward in a devastating way on the human community and was used to rank human beings themselves. In terms of gender, it credited the male of the species, naturally gifted with spirit and clear, calm reason, with being more godlike than the female of the species, identified with body and messy emotions. This supported the social hierarchy of men over women. Since men are more representative of God due to their superior intellects and ability to act—or so men philosophers and theologians said—they rightly rule over women who, being more emotional and body-oriented, exist with an inferiority for which there is no remedy. In addition, as birthgivers who bring forth new life out of their own bodies, women were also closely associated with nature itself, Mother Earth. Both women and nature were subordinated to men's rule, too often interpreted as dominance, which can turn violent and exploitative with little compunction.

This same framework turned even more vicious in the fifteenth and sixteenth centuries when Europeans began their vigorous exploration of other lands. Then thinkers in that aggressive entrepreneurial culture took human superiority to mean that explorers had the right to exploit the minerals, forests, and animals in other lands for profit. Even more toxic was the support this view gave to white Christian European men's idea of their own supremacy when they encountered African and Indigenous peoples. By assigning to people of color souls of lesser quality, an inferior intelligence, and a greater identification with bodiliness, Europeans thought they had the right to conquer, transport, and enslave millions of human beings for profit, without remorse. Given its commitment to the hierarchical view of the world, church teaching had little to offer by way of push-back or resistance to the devastating disruption of whole human communities and individual lives. The terrible racist results of slavery continue to this day.

It is daunting to realize how deeply this theory of the hierarchy of being has shaped Christian belief and practice. Its ingrained conviction of the superiority of some people over others prevented the Christian community from consistently advocating for equality and justice in the human community. With its conviction that humans are masters and rulers of nature, it also opened the door to centuries of unbridled exploitation of nature without protest from the churches, until recently.

To be clear: church teaching alone does not bear full responsibility. Powerful secular forces in society also promoted human authority over nature. The Enlightenment theory of progress, for example, understood human history as an ongoing project of emancipation from the natural world; freed from its constraints, man (as they wrote) could shape the rest of the world according to his own needs and pleasures. Again, Francis Bacon, sixteenth-century promoter of the scientific method, argued that man had the right to investigate nature and probe into its secrets the way the Inquisition questioned female witches by probing their orifices under torture. The industrial era's need for resources, driven by newly awakened human inventiveness and the desire for profit, rampaged through forests, rivers, and mountains. The point of our reflection is not that religion drove culture in this ecologically damaging direction, but that religion was complicit.

The lack of concern on the part of many Christian people for the devastation of the earth in our own day can be traced in part to the ongoing influence of this construct of the hierarchy of being. If humans are the most godlike and important creatures, why should our focus not remain on ourselves? If Earth and its living species are of little importance to God, why should they matter to people of faith? Why not use them as we please?

Consider the trees

I have found one thought experiment very effective in introducing sobriety to minds drunk on human supremacy. Start with the idea that in the hierarchy of being humans rank higher than trees. When we breathe, humans inhale oxygen and exhale carbon dioxide. In the presence of the sun trees do the opposite. As part of their life process of photosynthesis, they take in carbon dioxide and emit oxygen. Photosynthesis is responsible for producing a great amount of the oxygen content of the Earth's atmosphere. Take away trees, and humans would suffocate. Take away humans, and trees would do just fine (probably better, for we wouldn't be cutting them down). Who needs whom more? Which is more valuable? By what criterion? In view of the human need to breathe, the hierarchy of being based on matter-spirit dualism does not make sense.

What a profound conversion of mind and heart it takes to migrate away from the human right to dominate toward an understanding of the community of creation in which human beings, with our superb intelligence and powers of agency, take a responsible and loving place as kin amid the land, sea, and sky; among the camel, the herring, the egret, the ladybug, and the date palm.

Each creature of intrinsic value

A strong call in precisely this direction resounds from Pope Francis's letter *Laudato Si'*. At its center is a spiritual vision of our blue marble of a planet and all its inhabitants as God's beloved creation, belonging to God. We humans need to see ourselves not "as lords and masters, entitled to plunder the earth at will" (*LS* 2); not as relentless consumers, "unable to set limits on our immediate needs" (*LS* 11); not as ruthless exploiters dominating the world with "unrestrained delusions of grandeur" (*LS* 114). Rather, our times call for ***a new way of being human*** that enhances rather than diminishes the life of our fellow creatures.

To get there, this extraordinary letter subtly dismantles the hierarchy of being in favor of an interconnected community of creation. Let us ponder a few highlights. Returning to a biblical view, Pope Francis recognizes that he is contributing something new to longstanding Catholic teaching by insisting that "we are called to recognize that other living beings have a value of their own in God's eyes" (*LS* 69). Redefining what church doctrine had judged to be of lesser worth, he continues forthrightly: "In our time the Church does not simply state that other creatures are completely subordinated to the good of human beings, as if they had no worth in themselves and can be treated as we wish" (*LS* 69). Rather, "They have an intrinsic value independent of their usefulness. Each organism, as a creature of God, is good and admirable in itself; the same is true of the harmonious ensemble of organisms existing in a defined space and functioning as a system," that is, an ecosystem (*LS* 140).

Note the shift away from instrumental to intrinsic value. The language is deliberate. And why is this so, why do other creatures matter in themselves? Because God loves them. "God's love is the fundamental moving force in all created things.... Even the fleeting life of the least of beings is the object of God's love, and in its few seconds of existence, God enfolds it with affection" (*LS* 77). Commentators note that the pope may well have been thinking of mayflies. Once these small insects emerge from underground they have only a few brief hours to find a mate and lay eggs before they die. Here and gone so quickly, yet they are enfolded with God's affection. As are we all.

In this light Francis characterizes other creatures with strong religious markers. They are bearers of revelation, since each one "reflects in its own way a ray of God's infinite wisdom and goodness" (*LS* 69). Each is also a "locus of divine presence," a place where we can encounter God (*LS* 88).

Besides subverting the philosophical idea of the hierarchy of being, *Laudato Si'* also challenges how the Genesis 1 story of creation has been used to justify the human right to rule over nature. This is not only inadequate but also frankly wrong:

> Although it is true that we Christians have at times incorrectly interpreted the Scriptures, nowadays we must forcefully reject the notion that our being created in God's image and given dominion over the earth justifies absolute domination over other creatures. (*LS* 67)

Granted, as humans in the community of creation with unique capacities of knowledge, will and freedom, we do indeed have a special role, namely, to respect, protect, and care for the others with whom we share a common home. But we exercise this responsibility not outside of or above the network of living beings, but within it, sharing with other creatures in "one splendid universal communion" (*LS* 220) all created and loved by God.

In an interesting way *Laudato Si'* turns to the example of Jesus to buttress its critique of the hierarchy of being. Shaped by biblical faith in God the Creator, Jesus had a tangible and loving relationship with the natural world. He was not an ascetic set apart from the world, thinking one must turn away from the body and the Earth in order to have communion with God. To the contrary, his practices of eating and drinking led others to call him a drunkard and a glutton, as he himself acknowledged (Matt 11:19). In later times, unfortunately, some followers forgot this *joie de vivre.* By despising the body, both the human body and the body of nature, they literally did damage to the good news that Jesus came to bring. But:

> He was far removed from philosophies that despised the body, matter, and the things of the world. Such unhealthy dualisms, nevertheless, left a mark on certain Christian thinkers in the course of history and disfigured the gospel. (*LS* 98)

Disfigured the gospel! In the spirit of Jesus we need to turn back toward bodiliness, our own bodies and all bodies on earth, with love rather than rejection, for all are part of God's beloved creation.

Laudato Si' hammers home a final point about the natural world with a sweeping statement about the meaning of it all:

> The ultimate destiny of the universe is in the fullness of God. . . . The final purpose of other creatures is not to be found in us. Rather, all creatures are moving forward, with us and through us, towards a common point of arrival, which is God. (*LS* 83)

The inclusive, strongly ethical vision of this letter resonates with insight into what it means to call Earth the creation. Once we appreciate the value of the other, we arrive at a new starting point for ethical behavior.

Embedded

How shall we humans understand ourselves and our place among other living beings on the Earth? Does the good Creator want humans to dominate and exploit other living species? Clearly not. Are we called to be intelligent, responsible stewards? Yes, but not as if we are separate from the rest of creation. Are we basically brothers and sisters, meant to give and receive in the kinship of the community of creation? Yes, first and most fundamentally.

In this era of ecological devastation, the vocation of human beings to take faithful care of the Earth resounds with urgency. We need to be responsible! However, this does not presume an arrangement of the world with humans at the apex, vested with authority over all the rest. There are, of course, enormous differences among species. But what the hierarchy of being blocks from view is that first and foremost we are all beloved creatures of God, interrelated in the community of creation, dependent on each other for our very lives. We are all kin in the radiant tapestry of life. And we stand or fall together.

Let the word "God" bring the sparrows before our eyes—"not one of them is forgotten in God's sight" (Luke 12:6). Let divine affection that enfolds even tiny, seemingly insignificant insects come as a grace that challenges our species' arrogance, expands our humility, restores our sense of belonging to the community of creation, and inspires our own hearts' love.

All the ends of the earth have seen
the salvation by our God.
Sing joyfully to the vulnerable Lord, all you lands,
Break into song; sing praise.

—Psalm 98:3–4

24
Praying: we and us

May God be gracious to us and bless us.
—Psalm 67:1

Who is "us"?

Ask yourself: what comes to mind when you hear the pronouns "we" and "us" in a religious context? What do you see in your mind's eye when this pronoun is used in preaching or teaching, reading or writing, and when praying together with others or alone? May God have mercy on us, we say. May God bless us. May God's light shine upon us. Who is "us"? Almost always we see it referring to members of the human community, to "We the People," however narrowly or broadly we draw the boundaries of the group.

Imagine the change in awareness and practice if we understood that the reach of these pronouns includes the whole community of life. Given that we are all kin as creatures of God on the way to a redeemed final future, this would be the true thing to do. Widening the net would work to heal the affliction of our species blindness, a narrowness of vision that relegates the natural world to the periphery of spiritual interest and concern.

In our polarized human society today, it is already a challenge to expand the boundary of "us" beyond our own tribal silos to include humans who differ by race, gender, class, sexual orientation, immigration status, education, political opinion, religion, and other markers by which we shape our personal and group identities. Thankfully, the core teaching of Torah reframed by Jesus, to love your neighbor as yourself, exerts a constant pressure to go beyond the limits of our prejudice in order to love, respect, and do justice to *all* people. All human beings are included in "us."

In this ecological era, faith in God who enfolds all creatures with affection invites us to cross the species line and include other living creatures who are not *Homo sapiens* in "us." If there is one God, one holy mystery of love whose Spirit creates, indwells, and sustains all creatures, who enfolds all with affection, whose Word became flesh in Jesus Christ as part of the biosphere, this Jesus whose death on the cross puts him in solidarity with all living creatures that suffer and die, and whose resurrection promises a blessed future for the whole world, then "us" includes the whole community of creation.

An Extraordinary Species, Recently Arrived

It is inevitable that some will raise an objection based on the extraordinary powers of human consciousness, or the superior functioning of human mind and will, or the wonders of imagination and agency that appeared in the world with human beings. To be clear, in no way does this expansion of meaning imply that all species are the same. Our human distinctiveness, a real, if recent, element in the world, is amazing, valuable, and to be respected.

But consider this: for 99.99 percent of the time that has passed since the so-called Big Bang started the universe, there were no human beings at all. The universe is about 13.8 billion years old. Anatomically modern humans or *Homo sapiens*, our species, emerged on Earth somewhere between 300,000 and 200,000 years ago from prior species of human ancestors in Africa. To help our minds grasp this, the scientist Carl Sagan suggested a rough timeline that scales the history of the universe onto one Earth year. If the Big Bang took place on January 1, then our Milky Way galaxy formed on May 12. After the birth and death of generations of stars, our solar system formed on September 2. Primitive life forms began to grow on Earth on September 21, followed by multi-cellular organisms around November 15. The days of December saw a sequence of species emerge, ranging from worms, fish, land plants, insects, and amphibians, to trees, dinosaurs, mammals, birds, flowers, and hominids. Modern human beings emerged on December 31 at ten minutes to midnight.

We are young members of creation, a species only recently arrived. Yet in a short time we have developed a magnificent array of cultures marked by inventiveness and beauty but also by ugliness and evil. We have managed to figure out the main lines of the cosmic story that has led to our existence. We have also figured out how to make nuclear weapons whose use would destroy most of life on Earth. Tragically, our current use of fossil fuels is damaging the very climate that for thousands of years has made our planet so hospitable to the flourishing of life.

Clearly we are a species with uniquely powerful abilities to think, speak, and act, to build up and destroy. This is not to say whether intelligent life might or might not exist elsewhere. But anyone who would say that humans are equivalent to other creatures on Earth is blatantly ignoring the fact that we are the only species currently wreaking havoc on our planet. Yet it is also the case that human distinctiveness is embedded in a larger network of other lives. Let us ponder the connections.

KINSHIP BETWEEN ALL SPECIES

All creatures come from the hand of the one gracious God, are held in existence by the same vivifying Creator Spirit, and at the end will be gathered into a new heaven and a new earth by the same ineffable love. Put in other words, all creatures have their origin and future in the one holy God and exist in absolute reliance on divine life-giving power in every present historical moment. From this theocentric perspective, there is not one species over here and another over there. In our beautiful, terrible, fragile, and vulnerable lives, we all share the fundamental identity of belonging to the same generous God.

Christian theology develops this understanding further in light of Jesus Christ, in whom the Word of God became flesh, thus joining the evolutionary story at a particular historical moment. In his life, death, and resurrection, Jesus Christ entered into solidarity with all who live and suffer and die, in order to save from within. From this christological perspective, there is not one species over here and another over there. All together form one community of life on the way to being redeemed.

The scientific perspective, too, leads to this same insight. Endless forms most beautiful have evolved on the Earth. Yet undergirding the tremendous variation lies a profound interconnection forged by a shared history of biological descent with small changes made over deep time. The very materials that compose the land, water, and air out of which life evolved and continues to exist were themselves formed in the explosions of ancient stars. Scientifically there is not one species over here and another over there. There is but one planetary community of life.

Unity in difference

One of the spiritual practices *Laudato Si'* encourages is nurturing a feeling that we are "intimately united with all that exists" (*LS* 11). While not a familiar feeling to many of us, such a deep sense of connection is obviously in tune with both religious truth and scientific data. It is something we can aspire to. But be warned: After so many centuries of human-centered thinking, it is terribly hard to climb down from our self-assigned privileged position and re-envision ourselves related as kin with other creatures in our common home. We have lived so long dazzled by our own intelligence that such a basic change can be wrenching. We have to deconstruct the architecture of our imagination and the feelings of our heart and reconstruct the understanding of ourselves as a human species in a more inclusive, relational manner. The language of *conversion* of mind and heart does not exaggerate the magnitude of such a change.

The naturalist Henry Beston penned a resonant description of animals that moves us in this direction. In a famous passage that builds to deep insight he wrote:

> We need another and a wiser and perhaps a more mystical concept of animals. . . . We patronize them for their incompleteness, for their tragic fate for having taken form so far below ourselves. And therein do we err. For the animal shall not be measured by man. In a world older and more complete than ours, they move finished and complete, gifted with the extension of the senses we have lost or never attained, living by voices we shall never hear. They are not brethren, they are not underlings: they are other nations, caught with ourselves in the net of life and time, fellow prisoners of the splendour and travail of the earth.

That is one poetic way of putting it. While not endorsing a kinship relation between humans and animals (they are not brethren), Beston's view of animal integrity nevertheless connects us deeply as fellow travelers on the one Earth. Animal studies today strengthen this insight, giving details of how animals negotiate their lives with companions in social orders with codes and communications, solve problems, and respond to new situations. They are living beings with consciousness, intelligence, and feelings.

Let us pray

Bringing this sensibility to prayer means growing the concepts of "we" and "us" to include other creatures as we give praise and ask for God's blessing and help. Our praise joins the praise of all creation which was glorifying God long before we humans evolved. Our prayer for help with human needs gathers up all creatures in distress. The one big exception is asking for forgiveness of sin. There is no sin among animals, for this requires a kind of thinking that can distinguish right from wrong in a moral sense and a capacity to choose with a significant measure of freedom. Humans have a corner on this.

There is, however, suffering and death among animals, and striving for the necessities of a good life. With this in view, the prayer to God to have mercy on us all is beautifully apt. Biblical scholars point out that Hebrew word for mercy is a cognate of the word for a woman's womb. In Phyllis Trible's memorable words, the meaning of mercy traces the journey of a metaphor from the wombs of women to the compassion of God. "Have mercy on us" actually asks God to show compassion on us the way a mother shows love for the child of her womb: have womb-love on us, have fierce maternal care for us. In some situations mercy entails forgiving sin. At other times it involves protecting from harm, nurturing, giving what is needed for growth, teaching, disciplining, offering comfort in suffering, laughing, adding to joy. Have mercy on "us" comes to mean: may the whole Earth and all its creatures flourish. Praying with this sense of wide kinship effects an ever-expanding love in the human heart in response to the call of the living God whose love goes far beyond anything we can ask or imagine.

Psalm 67 provides a wonderful example of this sensibility in the very way it is structured. A short song of thanksgiving, it begins with a prayer for blessing: "May God be gracious to us and bless us," and it ends the same way: "May God continue to bless us." Who is the "us" in this prayer? The psalm unfolds with a remarkable rhetorical dynamic. As it opens, "us" refers to the people who are saying this prayer, originally the people of Israel and now the gathered community whom God blesses. But the psalmist believes that divine blessing on Israel is the means God uses to reveal divine blessing on all the nations. Mid-psalm this starts to happen: "Let the nations be glad and sing for joy," for God guides them also with justice and faithfulness. This obviously refers to divine guidance for human nations, but can just as well refer to cohorts of animals in Beston's sense. By the end of the psalm, a good harvest has come in and now the blessing extends to the whole earth:

> The earth has yielded its increase; God, our God, has
> blessed us.
> May God continue to bless us;
> and may all the ends of the earth revere God's holy
> name.

Imagine praying this psalm with the "us" expanded to the community of creation. Penguins, gorillas, woodpeckers, and sunflowers would be included in the blessing, their faces lit with divine favor as they go about their business. "May God continue to bless us" would mean all of us creatures, from the Arctic to the Antarctic, to the ends of the earth.

Making the option for an amplified "we" and "us" places the prayer of spiritual seekers and faith communities in relation to all the earth, its ecosystems and species, because that is where God is to be found. In union with the compassionate heart of God, we are inspired to enfold other creatures with our affection and act to save the earth under threat. Then care for our common home becomes not something added on, but part of loving our neighbor, loving "us."

Give us this day our daily bread.
—Matthew 6:11

God's Beloved Creation

25

Two books

Ask the beasts and they will teach you;
the birds of the air, and they will tell you;
ask the plants of the earth and they will teach you;
and the fish of the sea will declare to you.
Who among these does not know
that the hand of the bountiful Lord has done this?
In God's hand is the life of every living thing,
and the breath of every human being.

—Job 12:7–10

Isn't this a stunning invitation? Ask the animals, the birds, the plants, and the fish to teach us about God! This assumes they are repositories of religious knowledge. What could they possibly tell us? For one thing, they teach that their very being here at all is due to the Singer singing her song; their very existence points to God who makes them. For another, they declare that their vulnerable lives rest in God's hands through their flourishing and their dying, as (lest we forget) do the lives of humans who share the planet with them. All these rampantly different creatures on land, sea, and air bear witness to the creative love of God.

The insight that the natural world can teach us about its Creator arises from a healthy sense of creation. Created beings point to the One who made them. In the early centuries of Christian theology this gave rise to the vintage idea that there are *two* books that reveal something about the heart of holy mystery.

Two books

One book, obviously, is the Bible. This is a collection of stories, commandments, poetry, letters, prophecies, teachings, laws, histories, testimonies, and prayers written by various people using different languages in widely diverse circumstances over many centuries. Compiled into one book, the result is revered as inspired scripture that discloses truth about the one living God who creates, redeems, and sanctifies the world now and into the future. The holy book also makes clear how we human beings should live in response, by loving God with all our heart, soul, mind, and strength and by loving our neighbor as ourselves. Passages from this book are read publicly at every Mass. The people gathered for worship respond with gratitude: "Thanks be to God." The preacher gives homilies that draw out the meaning of its stories and teachings. Composers write hymns and prayers from its verses. Individuals pray and meditate on its texts. Breaking all records as the most translated book in the world, its message is conveyed to peoples of the most diverse cultures in over seven hundred languages, while sections have been translated into more than three thousand languages. What a treasure.

The other book of revelation is the book of nature. It can be called a revelation because the world too teaches us about its Maker. God gave us both books. We should learn to read them both in order to glimpse their author and learn how to walk the right path.

One advocate of this view was Augustine. Convinced of the creative presence of the Spirit of God in the world, he preached a memorable sermon on the subject:

> Others, in order to find God, will read a book. Well, as a matter of fact there is a certain great big book, the book of created nature. Look carefully at it top and bottom, observe it, read it. God did not make letters of ink for you to recognize him in; he set before your eyes all these things he has made. Why look for a louder voice? Heaven and earth cry out to you, "God made me." Yes, you can read what Moses wrote. But in order to write it, what did Moses read, a man living in time? Observe heaven and earth in a religious spirit.

What a keen insight, laced with humor. In those days it was thought that Moses had written the first five books of the Bible. Obviously, he himself had no prior books of scripture to read. So how did he learn about God? He observed the sky and the earth in a religious spirit. In other words, he read the book of nature. It taught him of the Creator's greatness and beauty and powerful, compassionate care. So we too should do.

A forgotten tradition

In ensuing centuries in the West, regrettably, the book of nature became widely neglected. Today when people gather for worship this book is barely ever mentioned. The congregation does not routinely thank God for it. Preachers do not break open the meaning of its words. Very few pastors or religious scholars are trained in how read or translate its text. In the house of prayer it lies closed and covered with dust.

The ecological challenges of our day make this silence particularly damaging. In general we lack a deep understanding of the religious meaning of the natural world that would motivate care of the Earth. Along with that, we lack the insight into the greatness and beauty of its author which nature could teach. It is time to open this book once again. As we do so, we find ourselves awash in advances in scientific knowledge that broaden the kinds of creatures we can ask.

Ask the galaxies

On July 11, 2022, the first full-color photograph of deep space taken by the new James Webb telescope was unveiled in a program televised from the U.S. White House. After traveling over one million miles into the cosmos, this incredibly powerful telescope had trained its lens on a patch of sky approximately the size of a grain of sand held at arm's length, a tiny speck of the vast universe. The picture it took revealed thousands of galaxies, including the faintest objects ever yet observed. Given the speed at which light travels, this picture also had us looking back in time, seeing the universe close to its beginning 13.8 billion years ago. There they were, these ancient galaxies, some just specks of light, some globular clusters, some whirling in their distinctive spiral dance like graceful ballerinas, some elongated into shimmering streaks by gravity.

In the early twentieth century, amid ongoing scientific controversy about the subject, we learned that our own spiral galaxy, called the Milky Way, is enormous, composed of billions of stars. Planet Earth revolves around one of them, our sun, located on an outer arm of the spiral. In quick order throughout the century we discovered that there are billions of other galaxies, each with its own billions of stars and planets. Intellectually and emotionally, we have hardly come to terms with such magnitude. Now the Webb telescope shows us thousands more galaxies existing in just one tiny spot in the universe. Multiply that out. How many galaxies are there in the universe altogether? When asked that question, the NASA scientist Bill Nelson, who gave the commentary at the photograph's unveiling, paused for a significant beat and could not hide his wonder: "Now the number is unlimited."

His choice of adjective astonished me. "Unlimited!" This verges on the infinite. Ordinarily scientists, committed to precise observation and data analysis, do not think that anything in the natural world is beyond measurement. Indeed, one can imagine that someday in the distant future, using this telescope and others yet to be designed, scientists may figure out the total number of galaxies. But for now, it is vaster than we can count.

Observe this Webb deep field photograph in a religious spirit. Here is another reminder of the fecundity of nature: thousands of galaxies, trillions of stars and unnumbered planets, a boundless realm of possibilities stretching back 13 billion years in a wee patch of sky. What kind of God created such a universe? Ask the galaxies to teach us. Glimpse the incomprehensible greatness of the Creator of galaxies, unlimited in number. "From the greatness and beauty of created things their original author, by analogy, is seen."

Ask a whale ecosystem

Not only the vastness of the heavens but also the intricacies of biological life on earth form part of the revelatory book of nature. Take, for example, baleen whales. These huge animals, including humpback, fin, blue, and minke whales, take in nourishment by filtering out vast amounts of ocean water through fringed baleen plates in their mouths and swallowing the prey that remains. This is mostly krill, a crustacean similar to a tiny shrimp. Back in the ocean the krill in turn feed on phytoplankton, microscopic plants that form the base of the food chain for many marine animals.

Tracking a group of tagged whales in 2022, scientists learned that the North Pacific blue whale, the largest animal on earth, consumes some 35,000 pounds of krill a day in the summer. The finding is important because whale feces are a critical source of nutrients in the open ocean. The more whale poop in the sea, the healthier the ecosystem and the more other species can thrive. By eating and digesting such enormous quantities of krill and then defecating, the blue whales release iron locked within the krill back into the water, making it available to phytoplankton that need the mineral to survive. The vital cycle runs from whale poop to healthy populations of phytoplankton to abundant krill to thriving numbers of animals including blue whales, singing their hauntingly beautiful songs deep in the sea.

Observe this complex, highly intricate ecosystem in a religious spirit. Ask the baleen whales to teach us. Glimpse the holy mystery of infinite relationality that is the creating source of such wide-ranging cooperative interaction. "From the greatness and beauty of created things their original author, by analogy, is seen."

One cannot meditate on this ecosystem without a shudder, remembering how commercial interests hunted some species of whales for their oil, meat, and baleen (used for fans and corsets), reducing whole species almost to extinction. By mid-twentieth century the blues in particular were almost exterminated. While making a slow comeback, this species is still listed today as endangered. Here the work of the author of beauty was close to ruined, with devastating impact on the surrounding ocean ecosystem. On the positive side of the ledger, it was human beings who finally called a halt to the hunt.

Learn to read

Just as the book of scripture has proved over the centuries to be a rich source of understanding the holy mystery of God, so too is the book of nature a source of enlightenment. The Creator Spirit dwells within all creation. In turn, creation reflects the author of its beauty and greatness, not without remainder, but with hints, clues, pointers. Knowledge of God is mediated through the vast diversity of creation. Let us learn to read each of the two books through the optics of the other. Observe heaven and earth in a religious spirit.

> *God heals the brokenhearted,*
> *and binds up their wounds;*
> *counts out the number of the stars,*
> *and calls each one by its name.*
> —Psalm 147:3-4

26
Biodiversity: dazzling, disappearing

For you have made all things, the heaven and the earth,
and all that is held within the circle of heaven;
you are the Creator of all.

—Esther 4:17

Diverse Species

The book of Job invites us to ask the beasts to teach us about the God who made them. Imagine you took up this invitation to interrogate animals and other living beings to hear their wisdom about their Creator. Say, in order to get a wide range of opinion, you tried to call upon every living thing, or at least one representative of every species on Earth. How many creatures would you need to contact? How many animals of the land, birds of the air, plants of the earth, and fish of the sea, to say nothing of insects, fungi, and microscopic one-celled creatures? Even a spoonful of productive farm soil contains millions of living microbes of thousands of species. Daunting!

While the exact number of species on the planet remains unknown, and while scientific ways of counting differ, as of this writing one widely reported study estimates that there are a total of 8.7 million known species, with about 6.5 million found on land and 2.2 million dwelling in water. There is widespread agreement that these figures fall far short of the actual number of species on Earth. Many, especially in the smaller range, have not yet been discovered or studied.

Bat, cat, rat, dog, pig, fox, baboon . . . blackbird, blue jay, goldfinch, scarlet macaw, white-tailed cockatoo, red-tailed hawk . . . daisy, rose, petunia, poppy, lilac, buttercup, crocus . . . ant, bee, cockroach, fly, butterfly, wasp . . . eel, bass, trout, swordfish, tuna, cod . . . apple tree, oak, maple, willow, magnolia, redwood . . . on and on. Truly, "the earth is full of your creatures" (Ps 104:24).

This vast array came into existence slowly over millions of years by the process of evolution. Now Earth is adorned with more than 10,000 species of birds spread across every continent. Over 4,000 kinds of lizards. Over 34,000 different types of fish in the sea. And who can forget British biologist J. B. S. Haldane's quip that if a god or divine being had created all living organisms on Earth, then that creator must have an "inordinate fondness for beetles," given that there are about 300,000 species of them.

Each species inhabits an ecological niche that supplies it with nourishment and shelter. Each draws from and gives back to the land, water, and air of its habitat. Interacting with other organisms in its geographic area, each forms an integral part of an ecosystem such as wetland, forest, desert, mountain, seashore, tundra, prairie, coral reef, even city. In this setting, each performs the vital task of bringing forth the next generation. Taken all together, the different species create a network of life that circles the globe and is the distinguishing feature of our planet.

Refracting goodness

To Job's way of seeing, these different creatures in their beauty, their variety, their interacting, their coming to be and passing away bear witness to the overflowing goodness of their Creator who gives life and breath to all mortal flesh. Musing about why there is such a teeming diversity of creatures to begin with (even to the medieval European eye there were quite a few), Aquinas concluded that their very difference, bug from catfish from human from skylark from cheetah, is necessary to express divine goodness:

> For God brought things into being in order that divine goodness might be communicated to creatures, and be represented by them; and because this goodness could not be adequately represented by one creature alone, the Creator produced many and diverse creatures, that what was wanting to one in the representation of the divine goodness might be supplied by another. For goodness, which in God is simple and uniform, in creatures is manifold and divided. Hence the whole universe together participates in the divine goodness more perfectly, and represents it better than any single creature whatever.

In this religious perspective, what today is called biodiversity manifests in its own natural way the abounding generosity of the living God. At the same time, the relationship of creation whereby various creatures reflect the goodness of God is the basis for any speech about holy mystery at all, for in knowing the excellence of the world we may speak indirectly but truly about the one Creator whose greatness and beauty it reflects.

Note how this insight about creatures reflecting divine goodness validates the importance of the diversity of species. Denis Edwards explains:

> No one creature, not even the human, can image God by itself. Only the diversity of life—huge soaring trees, the community of ants, the flashing colors of the parrot,

> the beauty of a wildflower, along with the human—can give expression to the radical diversity and otherness of the trinitarian God.

In the simple words of *Laudato Si'*, each creature "reflects in its own way a ray of God's infinite wisdom and goodness" (*LS* 69). How much more does the whole ensemble together reflect the glory of God!

Going extinct

As a natural part of the evolutionary process, one species or another goes extinct over time. It comes to end of the arc of its resourcefulness and peters out. The opening leaves room for some other creature to move in and develop. Over millions of years the natural background rate of extinction has been about one to five species per year. Keep that number in mind.

In addition to this slow vanishing of species, Earth has also experienced five catastrophic events of mass extinction. Mass extinction happens when a change of environment is too rapid and widespread for species to be able to adapt. The conditions for staying alive became so treacherous that the majority of species die out. The most recent wipe-out occurred about 65 million years ago when a gigantic asteroid crashed into Earth near what today is Mexico's Yucatan Peninsula. The impact threw enormous quantities of dust and particles into the atmosphere, resulting in a winter that lasted for decades. The prolonged darkness and cold wiped out nearly all non-flying dinosaurs and more than half of all other species then existing. It took tens of millions of years for nature to rebound to the plenitude of life that our planet is known for today.

In our day, Earth is experiencing what many are calling a sixth mass extinction of species. According to a 2019 landmark

United Nations study, more than one million animal and plant species are threatened with extinction in the coming decades. Earth is currently experiencing its largest loss of species since the dinosaurs. Such a dangerous thinning out of the natural world has not happened before in all the time that the species *Homo sapiens* has existed on the planet.

This time the asteroid is us. Humans are changing the atmosphere, destroying habitats, and consuming the natural resources of land and sea with such magnitude and speed that it is becoming impossible for other species to adapt and survive. As a result, whole species (not just individuals) are disappearing by the thousands. Consider these key drivers of species death. We have overfished the oceans, cut down great tropical forests, and converted massive grasslands and prairies to agricultural use for crops and livestock. We have produced waste that pollutes water sources and fouls the air and used pesticides that poison the soil and kill beneficial insects. We have built cities and highways, constructed fences and dammed rivers in ways that crowd out natural habitats, fragment biological corridors, and disrupt migratory patterns. Over all these destructive activities looms global warming caused by human use of fossil fuels, which is disrupting life-cycles in dire ways.

For a time Earth could replenish its physical resources after increased human use, but no longer. We are depleting the riches of ecosystems at too rapid a rate. For a time other species could largely regrow their populations after human predation, but no longer. Demand for economic growth along with our habits of consuming are putting too much pressure on their reproductive success. With their habitats disappearing, plants and animals are running out of room and resources. Estimates vary widely, but the rate of extinction now stands at upwards of hundreds of species a day, as compared to the natural historical erasure of one to five a year.

The death of birth

Let us face the awesome reality of extinction. When a species goes extinct, it is not just an individual that dies but a particular lineage, a unique configuration of pulsing life that emerged through the process of evolution and exists with a unique grace in the ecological community. What is horrifying is that when a species goes extinct it can never come back. There are no more babies, no more eggs, no more seeds. The disappearance is irreversible. Given that evolution requires a flow of genes from past ancestor to future progeny, their kind is cut off with a finality that brings down the curtain. "Death cuts off life; extinction cuts off birth," in Jonathan Schell's memorable words. A tear is ripped in the planet's fabric of life. We should be holding funerals.

The disappearance of species usually happens quietly. They simply die off from habitat loss, pollution, or food shortages. One young scientist told of sighting an endangered migratory bird, the Bachman's warbler, on a creek in Virginia. To his astonishment, he had no trouble hearing and then seeing the bird. A full-plumaged male, it sat on an open branch about twenty feet up and hardly stopped singing during the two hours it was observed. The extraordinary exertions of this bird were a sign that he was in prime breeding condition and was singing to attract a mate. But no female ever responded to his call. Environmental stress had reduced their numbers and spread them out too thinly over their range. The Bachman's warbler has not been spotted for over forty years, and is now considered extinct. Just like that, it is silently gone.

Already in the twenty-first century, species of ibex, cougar, rhinoceros, tortoise, frog, tree snail, woodpecker, and leopard have gone extinct, along with species of Hawaiian birds, mussels and freshwater fish, and various types of shrubs, flowers, and grasses. You can google "species extinction/current year" and compose your own Book of the Dead.

Religious meaning

Recognizing the tragedy of these vanished creatures, *Laudato Si'* makes a startling religious claim about extinction:

> Each year sees the disappearance of thousands of plant and animal species which we will never know, which our children will never see, because they have been lost forever. The great majority become extinct for reasons related to human activity. Because of us, thousands of species will no longer give glory to God by their very existence, nor convey their message to us. We have no such right. (*LS* 33)

By making species go extinct, we humans are not only destroying unique, beautiful, important creatures that are key parts of the web of life on this planet. We are also silencing praise of God. And we are erasing religious knowledge about the Creator of us all.

Note the strong ethical commitment that this religious teaching calls forth. If religious folk truly grasped that extinction dims the glory of God on Earth and erases nature's revelatory message, that conviction could unleash a powerful force for protection. Pressing home the point, *Laudato Si'* describes how ruination should affect us: "God has joined us so closely to the world around us that we can feel the soil drying out into desert almost as a physical ailment, and the extinction of a species as a painful disfigurement" (*LS* 89). What an extraordinary idea. The loss of a species should strike us as if our own body had been wounded, as if we ourselves had lost a limb.

JOINING OUR EFFORTS

One would think that sheer human self-interest would galvanize efforts to halt the erasure. A strong assembly of millions of species millions of years in the making has caused Earth to be a richly productive place, hospitable to the thriving of the human species. A cumulative loss of species begins to rip apart this life-support system and threatens human well-being now and into the future. The damage afflicts harm on Indigenous Peoples with their spiritual and cultural connection to the land. It threatens the livelihood of billions of people who rely on wild species for food, fuel, and income. And it weakens every ecosystem on which all of us humans depend for our very life. In the words of the UN Secretary-General in 2022, "We are committing suicide by proxy."

Mass extinction is not inevitable. Human beings are causing it and we can do something about it. An increasing number of scientists, activists, young and old concerned citizens, government officials, economists, humanists, poets and artists are stepping up to protect the natural world. Meditating on biodiversity now under dangerous threat, lovers of God can draw on a profound wellspring of energy to join in the defense of our kin in the community of creation. The ecological commitment arising from belief in God and the love of our one heart can be a powerful force that, together with others, can help to stem the tide.

There is the sea, great and wide;
creeping things innumerable are there,
living things both small and great.

—Psalm 104:25

27

Comfort the land

For God will comfort Zion,
will comfort all her waste places,
and will make her wilderness like Eden,
her desert like a garden.
—Isaiah 51:3

Comfort! Of all the ways to envision divine love at work amid ecological devastation, this one is a stunner. God will comfort the wasteland and turn it into a garden. What a beautiful idea.

Among humans

Let us begin with the meaning of comfort in human experience. At different times every human being needs comfort, for no one's life is without difficulty. In a special way we speak of comfort when people are ill or grieving the death of a loved one, or when they have failed at an important task or suffered trauma. To comfort means to soothe and console them. It may take the form of a bowl of homemade soup or some heartfelt words of support. At times simply being present is enough. In public calamities with a wide scope, comfort may take the form of volunteering or donating time or resources to help survivors, or taking political action to prevent a recurrence. The point is to ease distress, alleviate pain, strengthen hope amidst loss, encourage resilience, and by doing so to make room for good cheer, eventually.

In the scroll of Isaiah

The announcement that the Holy One will comfort the waste places arises in Isaiah specifically in the aftermath of war. Israel has been defeated. Fields of crops have been destroyed and cities burned. Not a stone is left upon a stone of the great temple in Jerusalem. Much of the nation's citizenry has been marched off to exile in a foreign country. The situation is desperate.

The prophetic word rings out to the human community: "Comfort, O comfort my people, says your God" (Isa 40:1). The call to comfort heralds the news that soon a new king will take over and the exiles will be allowed to return home. Rebuilding can begin. Ordinarily, comfort is not the first thing that comes to mind to describe the experience of war ending, oppression lifting, and people being liberated to put their lives back together. But what a beautiful way to describe intense suffering giving way to peace and the beginning of ordinary life. It makes even nature glad:

> Sing for joy, O heavens, and exult, O earth;
> break forth, O mountains, into singing!
> For God has comforted the troubled people,
> and will have compassion on those who are suffering.
> (Isa 49:13)

It is not only defeated people in mourning who need comfort. The land, too, violated by being burned, uprooted, trampled, also needs consoling. The living God's lifeline of comfort turns also to the earth:

> For God will comfort Zion,
> will comfort all her waste places
> and will make her wilderness like Eden,
> her desert like a garden;
> joy and gladness will be found in her,
> thanksgiving and the voice of song. (Isa 51:3)

Maternal love

Isaiah's imagination forges a strong connection between God's giving comfort to war-torn people along with their ravaged land and the love a mother gives to her child. Today we would be quick to add that a loving father also comforts his child, as do grandparents and members of an extended family, and indeed any adult charged with the care of young members of our species.

Perhaps you can recall being a little child fortunate enough to be cared for by a loving adult. Sooner or later you will experience a most basic kind of consolation. If you fall down, your mom kisses the bruise and makes it feel better. If you wake up with a nightmare, your dad turns on the light, calms your fear, and makes the night safer. If another child takes away your toy, hits you, or unfairly wins the game, your *abuela* hugs you, and soothes you. They all wipe away tears from your little face and ease you into a better moment.

Focusing on the maternal relationship, Isaiah dares to call upon such intimate moments with vulnerable little ones to describe God's loving intent when bent over trouble:

> As a mother comforts her child,
> so I will comfort you. (Isa 66:13)

There are a million different ways mothers give comfort to their children every day—feeding, holding, caressing, encouraging, explaining, laughing, correcting, providing security, just being there as one who loves them, and so much more. Such deep and kind attentiveness is a powerful force that grows children into loving adults in their own right. On a broader scale it helps shape a society that functions with empathy. With this valuable experience in view, the prophet insists:

> But Zion said, "God has forsaken me;
>   my sweet Lord has forgotten me."
> Can a woman forget her nursing child
>   or show no compassion for the child of her womb?
> Even if these might forget,
>   I will not forget you. (Isa 49:14–15)

You could hardly think of a more tender expression of fiercely maternal divine love. The great Mother God, source of all mother love, remains faithful beyond all human possibility, comforting the people, comforting the land.

Comfort the earth

Human disasters, especially war, lay waste to whole swaths of territory. Land, waters, and air are fouled by human-caused pollution. Commercial interests cut down, dig out, blow up, and otherwise ruin living ecosystems for profit. Looming over all else in our day is global warming, which is creating havoc everywhere you look.

What an extraordinary chord this idea of God wanting to comfort the ravaged earth strikes in our ecologically troubled time. The divine Comforter inspires our participation. End pollution of the river: comfort the waters. Stop burning fossil fuels: comfort the atmosphere. Cut back pesticides, plant trees, clean the beach, reclaim empty city lots for community gardens: comfort the land. Vote into political office those who will make and honor climate agreements: comfort the whole Earth. The wonderfully poignant reality of God comforting the waste places calls us into partnership with divine love to strengthen and repair the earth.

> *As a mother comforts her child,*
> *so I will comfort you.*
> —Isaiah 66:13

28
The rock of my heart

God alone is my rock and my salvation.
—Psalm 62:2

Building on the teaching in Genesis 1 that human beings are made in the image and likeness of God, the Jewish and Christian traditions have long spoken about God with images and relationships taken from human experience. Given the patriarchal context of these traditions, images of God as a lord, king, or father predominate. But there are also references to God that draw on the role of a woman in labor, midwife, mother who comforts and protects, Holy Wisdom, shepherd, liberator, potter, lover, friend, builder, and many more. In this meditation we reflect on how another member of the community of creation which is not human, namely rock, can rightly represent the living God.

God our rock

Why call God a rock? Rocks are so impersonal, unfeeling, just unmoving chunks of heavy, solidified minerals, not even alive. Of all created things, they seem among the least apt for speaking about the dynamic wellspring of being that empowers everything and loves the world with a passion we cannot begin to fathom. But consider what rock has to offer.

Rock is the basic element of which the solid Earth is composed. As bedrock it supports all life above it on land and in the sea. Geologists teach that there are three basic types, which shift and change in a continuous rock cycle over long periods of time. Igneous rock forms from fiery molten magma deep within the hot Earth. Sometimes it spews forth from volcanoes and flows as lava; at other times it crystallizes and rises to the surface, granite being a good example. Sedimentary rock like sandstone forms when grains of minerals are compacted together under pressure, usually at the bottom of a body of water. Metamorphic rock such as marble results when the first two types alter their form under the force of high heat or pressure. However it comes into being, most rock has the quality of being firm, hard, solid, and enduring.

It is just this character that renders rock an excellent reference point for God. As Martin Luther described it, God is the one on whom you lean your heart, the one on whom your heart relies, the one whom you can trust. Can the one on whom you lean support all the complexity of your heart or will this one crumble under the weight of your life? The parable Jesus told of two houses, one built on rock and the other on sand, makes the point in a picturesque manner. When rain, floods, and wind beat on the houses, the first stood firm while the other collapsed (Matt 7:24–27). Rock is where you want to build.

In scripture the reference to God as a Rock is usually connected with salvation or deliverance from harm. There is appeal to God in time of trouble:

> To you, O God, I call; my rock, do not be deaf to me.
> (Ps 28:1)

And there is praise when one is rescued from enemies:

> The faithful Lord lives! Blessed be my rock!
> Exalted be my God, the rock of my salvation.
> (2 Sam 22:47)

The geography of the land of Israel, which is rocky and hilly, gives good reason for the reference. If someone was fleeing from an enemy, they might hide out in a cave hewn from rock or find safety in an impregnable fortress made from rock. In and through that particular circumstance, the notion of God the Rock who is strong and reliable and can save took on its own meaning.

We get some idea of how rock inspired thoughts of divine reliability in a biblical song that declares, "I will proclaim the name of the bountiful Lord, praise the greatness of our God, the Rock," and goes on to describe the Rock as one whose work is without fault, whose ways are just, who is faithful and without deceit, who is kind and upright (Deut 32:3–4). What excellent characteristics! The Rock is just, faithful, honest, true, full of integrity, genuinely good. You get the feeling you can lean on a God like this.

Again and again the scriptures show that the great living God who made heaven and earth has an eye for those on the periphery of privilege and a heart for justice that will make things right. This characteristic comes to the fore when the weight of the Rock tips the scales toward the lowly. We see this in the lovely canticle of Hannah, sung when she bore a much-desired child after years of yearning. Presenting him to God's service she sang:

> There is no Holy One like the generous Lord, no one besides you;
> there is no Rock like our God. (1 Sam 2:2)

Her own reversal of fortune gave her insight into how this Rock operates. God breaks the bows of the mighty, she sang, but strengthens the feeble; sends the rich out to work but fattens up the hungry; raises up the poor from the dust and sits them with princes; brings low and also exalts. No wonder her spirit rejoiced.

You might note that the term "rock," rather than being used of God in an off-putting, objective way, summons up an intensely personal relationship: You are my rock, my rock and my redeemer, my rock of refuge, our saving rock, "my God, the rock of my salvation" (Ps 89:26). The reality of rock summons up such strength that calling upon God this way gives voice to an almost inexpressible trust at the core of a person's life. "My flesh and my heart may fail, but God is the rock of my heart and my portion forever" (Ps 73:26). God will be there for me, and for us, no matter what.

The sequence of sentiments in Psalm 31 has particular resonance for those who follow Jesus. The one who prays this psalm is in trouble and cries to God for help: "In your righteousness deliver me." The plea intensifies: "Be a rock of refuge for me, a strong fortress to save me." Then in a profound spirit of faith, this sufferer cedes all:

> You are indeed my rock and my fortress;
> for your name's sake lead me and guide me;
> free me from the net they have set for me,
> for you are my refuge.
> Into your hands I commend my spirit;
> you will redeem me, O Lord, faithful God.
> (Ps 31:3–5)

In Luke's version of the crucifixion, a dying Jesus prayed this same psalm:

> Then Jesus, crying out with a loud voice, said, "Father, into your hands I commend my spirit." Having said this, he breathed his last. (Luke 23:46)

The One whom Jesus called "*Abba*," father, was his rock, his fortress, his refuge. Jesus died in agonized trust that his God was faithful all the way down.

Ponder the faithfulness of God the Rock. Picture the bedrock that supports the enormous weight of the tall buildings in Manhattan. Think of the great granite formation called Half Dome in Yosemite National Park. Take the measure of the blocks of white marble that form the Lincoln Memorial in Washington DC. Hold the pebbles or small rocks you may have picked up from places you have visited. Recall a mountain you have seen or a park with an outcropping of rock used for climbing.

Lean.

> *I love you, O God, my strength.*
> *The faithful Lord is my rock, my fortress, and my deliverer,*
> *my God, my rock in whom I take refuge.*
>
> —Psalm 18:1–2

29
Under your wings

Be merciful to me, O God; be merciful to me,
for in you my soul takes refuge;
in the shadow of your wings I will take refuge,
until the destroying storms pass by.
Psalm 57:1

Let us linger over birds. While scripture speaks about God as a lion, a leopard, a mother bear, and other wild animals, it presses birds into service to evoke the holy mystery of God more than any other creature in the animal kingdom. If you can recall watching a bird at close range or stopping to admire a flock in flight, however briefly, bringing that memory to mind can enrich this meditation.

Flying

Except for the flightless ones, what marks birds as distinct animals is that they are not totally earth-bound. They can fly. With marvelous agility they spread their wings, rise up, move around the sky, and set down again, landing safely on branch, pond, field, or sidewalk. It is a marvel! In addition, many species of birds migrate with the changing seasons. Attuned to the magnetic field of the Earth, using cues from the sun and the stars and guided by geographic landmarks, they fly hundreds or even thousands of miles from breeding to wintering grounds driven mainly by the availability of food. What a wonder!

Singly or in flocks, bird flight awakens a sense of freedom, of uplift, of something transcendent beyond our design or control. Even in this era of human flight in airplanes and rocket-fueled space capsules, birds just naturally go where we cannot. Their flight is amazing. One description by the American environmentalist Aldo Leopold has become justly famous. The "sky dance" of the midwestern woodcock, performed in spring as a mating ritual, begins at sunset when the bird alights on bare ground and begins his peenting call.

> Suddenly the peenting ceases and the bird flutters skyward in a series of wide spirals, emitting a musical twitter. Up and up he goes, the spirals steeper and smaller, the twittering louder and louder, until the performer is only a speck in the sky. Then, without warning, he tumbles like a crippled plane, giving voice in a soft liquid warble that a March bluebird might envy. At a few feet from the ground he levels off and returns to his peenting ground, usually to the exact spot where the performance began, and there resumes his peenting.

The drama goes on for an hour, and at dawn the whole show is repeated. Where is the female? Does the bird succeed in mating? Answers are not immediately obvious. But the dancers in the sunset sky refute the theory that the main purpose of a game bird is to serve as food for humans.

The English poet Gerard Manley Hopkins felt a similar exaltation early one morning when he watched a falcon ride the wind. Catching air currents, the bird went rolling, hovering, swooping, its wings glinting in the rising sunlight:

> My heart in hiding
> Stirred for a bird—the achieve of, the mastery of the
> thing!

A flying bird seems to have slipped the bonds of Earth and to exist, however briefly, in a dimension beyond what confines us. Little wonder that when scripture tells the story of the Hebrew people's exodus from slavery it draws on this kind of imagery. Escaping from Egypt was like hitching a ride on a bird's great wings toward freedom. As the liberating God later reminds them: "I bore you up on eagles' wings and brought you to myself" (Exod 19:4).

Doves and the Spirit of God

One flying bird in particular has come to represent the Spirit of God in the Christian tradition, namely the dove. Usually imagined flying downward, the descent of the dove signifies divine blessing coming "down" from heaven to bring new life. This connection between God's Spirit, the dove, and the grace of new beginnings is writ large in the gospel accounts of Jesus's baptism. After coming up from the water, he was praying when heaven was opened "and the Spirit descended upon him in bodily form like a dove" (Luke 3:22).

Behind this scene lies a widespread practice in Near Eastern religions of treating the dove as an iconic representative of female deity. Whole flocks of these cooing birds were tended in cultic towers and sculpted into small clay shrines for devotees. They symbolized the attributes of love, beauty, and fecundity associated with female deities such as the Greek goddess Aphrodite. Now at Jesus's baptism this beaked and feathered avian being, God on the wing, so to speak, comes to signal divine blessing on Jesus, inaugurating his loving, fruitful ministry to the suffering and brokenhearted world.

It is interesting to note how strongly the imagery of the dove has pervaded the Christian imagination. The story of Pentecost describes the Spirit of God coming upon all the disciples in two forms, rushing wind and tongues of fire (Acts 2:2–3). No mention is ever made of a dove. Yet it is hard to recall even one artistic depiction of the Pentecost scene in fresco, painting, or stained glass window without a dove hovering over all.

Upwards toward freedom. Downwards with blessing. The flying bird, an animal face of God, radiates association with the free-moving Spirit, gracious and merciful.

Nesting

The reproductive behavior of birds offers another rich source of reflection. In the spring a mating pair gathers local materials and builds a nest. Once the eggs are laid the mating pair take turns incubating, sitting for hours, days and nights on end, the female more than the male, in all kinds of weather, even snow. When the chicks hatch, the work of satisfying their insatiable young appetites begins. Parents ferry insects, rodents, fish, and other prey to the nest and thrust the nourishment down the chicks' gaping throats. When the time comes to fly, parents flutter above the nest to stir their fledglings into action. This description does not fit every species of bird, but it describes what is generally the case.

In our day live cams bring this process right to our screens. From the tiny cups of hummingbirds to the giant structures of eagles, a camera trained on the nest can transmit the goings-on in real time with no humans present. It is well worth your time in the spring to click on the same link every day and spend a few minutes observing the story of one nest. From the endless hours of quiet brooding to the wee fuzzy hatchlings with open beaks, to their feathers growing and little wings fluttering, to their flying away and the empty nest, the way birds bring forth the next generation to their gracefulness in the skies is awesome. (Go to explore.org/livecams to see cameras trained on a variety of species; falcon and eagle live cams are plentiful around the United States).

The maternal imagery of the brooding bird finds lovely play in Augustine's riff on the creation story of Genesis 1. In the beginning when all was waste and void, the Spirit of God was *moving/blowing/hovering/sweeping/fluttering* over the waters. Given the nuance of the verb in play, he wrote, this could also mean that the Spirit of God was brooding over the water the way birds brood over their eggs, "where that warmth of the mother's body in some way also supports the forming of the chicks through a kind of influence of her own kind of love." The notion of a bird fostering and cherishing the growth of her young, actually engendering them into existence by the loving power of her own warm body, provides a striking animal image for the creative work of the Spirit, Giver of life.

Early Christianity carried forward the connection between the generative mother bird and the Holy Spirit with vigor. Some theologians noted how besides empowering Jesus into mission at his baptism, the Spirit overshadowed Mary to begin with, mothering Jesus into life at his conception in her womb (how many depictions of the Annunciation include the hovering dove although, as with Pentecost, there is no mention of this in scripture). The Spirit again gives Jesus new life in the resurrection. This same Holy Spirit brings believers to birth out of the watery womb of the baptismal font and, after birthing them, nourishes, protects, comforts, and leads them into the future, all actions of her divine maternal care. In one existing prayer from the early church in Syria, the individual believer meditates:

> As the wings of doves over their nestlings,
> And the mouths of their nestlings toward their mouths,
> So also are the wings of the Spirit over my heart.

The Syriac community also used the dove symbol in a social sense. In one liturgical prayer they appealed to the Holy Spirit for a world in trouble:

> The world considers you a merciful mother.
> Bring with you calm and peace,
> and spread your wings over our sinful times.

The doctrine of the motherhood of the Spirit carried in the image of the mother bird fostered a spirituality characterized by great warmth expressed in private and public prayer.

Protecting

Assimilating birds' protective care of their young into an understanding of divine help and protection, scripture draws explicitly on the life-guarding function of wings. These adult appendages of feather and bone protect chicks from weather extremes like blazing sun, strong wind, or driving rain. They also provide cover when predators attack. When the psalms pray, "Hide me under the shadow of your wings" (17:8); or let me "find refuge under the shelter of your wings" (61:4); or "You have been my help, and in the shadow of your wings I sing for joy" (63:7), they summon a sense of powerful divine protection in avian terms.

It makes sense that living within this tradition Jesus expressed his yearning to shield his people from destruction by portraying himself as a mother bird. His lament is poignant:

> Jerusalem, Jerusalem, the city that kills the prophets and stones those who are sent to it! How often have I desired to gather your children together as a hen gathers her brood under her wings, and you were not willing. (Matt 23:37)

Liturgical prayers call Jesus the lamb of God sacrificed to take away the sin of the world. These could well be supplemented with prayers to Jesus the mother hen, desirous of protecting the chicks with her own body, to make their future possible. In the eleventh century the brilliant theologian Anselm of Canterbury composed just such a prayer with deep emotional overtones:

> But you too, good Jesus, are you not also a mother?
> Are you not a mother who like a hen gathers her chicks
> beneath her wings? . . .
> And you, my soul, dead in yourself,
> run under the wings of Jesus your mother
> and lament your griefs under his feathers.
> Ask that your wounds may be healed
> and that, comforted, you may live again.
> Christ, my mother, you gather your chickens under
> your wings;
> This dead chicken of yours puts himself under those
> wings. . . .
> Warm your chicken, give life to your dead one, justify
> your sinner.

Mother Jesus's wings over the chicks are high and wide and all encompassing. They are there forever in love, but the chick is free beneath them to be its flawed self at its best and worst. The wings give no constriction but comfort, safeguard, and further the chick's life.

The ways of creatures can give us a glimpse of their Creator. In some of their typical behaviors birds provide a link to the broad tradition of divine maternal nurturing and care. What must it feel like to be a young bird, hatched into being by the warmth of your mother's body and able to take refuge under her sheltering wings? Safety, warmth, and protection from danger wash over the chick in that dark, feathery, comforting place.

Imagine that experience. Take shelter. Pray God spread her merciful wings over our planet being ravaged. Join in the protective action.

> *How precious is your steadfast love, O God!*
> *All people may take refuge in the shadow of your wings.*
>
> —Psalm 36:7

30

Come, have breakfast

The eyes of all look to you,
and you give them their food in due season.
You open your hand,
and satisfy the desire of every living thing.
—Psalm 145:15–16

"Come, have breakfast" (John 21:12). After calling out this invitation, Jesus served up a morning meal of bread and fish that had been cooking over a charcoal fire burning on the beach. Let us ponder these three simple words. Their dynamic opens a portal into an ecological image of the living God active with cordial hospitality toward all creatures, willing their good, wanting all to be fed.

The Story

The breakfast scene is embedded in a post-resurrection story at the end of John's gospel. The place is the shore of the Sea of Galilee. The time is daybreak. Seven disciples have gone out in a boat and fished all night but caught nothing. Jesus stands on the beach. At his direction they cast their nets again and make a huge catch of fish, one hundred fifty-three all told. After they land the boat "Jesus said to them, 'Come, have breakfast.'... Jesus came and took the bread and gave it to them and did the same with the fish."

It is the risen Jesus whom the story depicts engaged in the mundane action of preparing and serving breakfast. The prophet from Nazareth whom the disciples had left their livelihoods to follow was no longer with them in the same way as during the days of his ministry. He had been put to death. A victim of unjust violence inflicted by the state, he suffered under Pontius Pilate, was crucified, died, and was buried. The unexpected, surprising, practically unbelievable good news that the gospel tells in story form is that death did not have the final word. Raised to new transformed life by the creative power of God, he now shows himself to the disciples from the other side of death. Like the other resurrection narratives in the gospels, this one reveals that the crucified Jesus is alive in God and present in a new way through the power of the Spirit.

The Story Interpreted

Given his exalted status, it may seem odd that Jesus, now being confessed as the Christ or Messiah, the Son of God and the Word of God, would be busy with the routine details of preparing and serving breakfast. Commentaries written by most theologians and biblical scholars across the centuries give short shrift to this behavior, if indeed they address it at all. Their interest focuses more intently on the marvelous catch of fish, or the number 153 which represents the number of nations whom the disciples are sent to "catch" with the gospel. Many Catholic interpreters dwell at even more length on the exchange after breakfast when Peter, who had denied Jesus three times during his trial, makes a threefold confession of love and receives the mandate to "Feed my lambs... Feed my sheep." Traditional interpretations of this appearance story tend to focus more on the authority of Peter and his papal successors in the institutional church than on Jesus's words and actions around breakfast. Not many attend to the job description that would have Peter become the chief nurturer, the feeder-in-chief.

There is a little grey brick church on the shore of the Sea of Galilee where the breakfast-at-sunrise gospel is commemorated. My own experience of visiting the place was a bit jarring. Among pilgrim groups it is customary to read the relevant gospel story while en route to different sites. With the words of Jesus's invitation to breakfast fresh in my mind and delighting my spirit, we arrived to learn that the building is called the Church of the Primacy of Saint Peter. Plaques pay tribute to visits to the site by Pope Paul VI and Pope John Paul II, successors of Peter. However, this church could more suitably bear a name that calls attention to Jesus's action of feeding. A certain gender bias may explain why this is not the case.

The Church of Jesus Making Breakfast

While gender roles are shifting in many places around the world, it is still the case that the majority of breakfasts on any given day are prepared by women—mothers, grandmothers, wives, school cafeteria workers, care-givers to the elderly, and more. For sure, some men perform this service in a superb manner whether at home for their partners and children, in commercial establishments, or at other locales where men predominate, such as the military and fire houses. Yet getting breakfast ready is still largely the unpaid or low-wage work of women around the world. Although such daily work keeps everyone alive and revved up for the day, it is easily overlooked when the contender for attention is the structural power of an institution run by men.

But let us attend to the story. The widely overlooked detail of the risen Jesus busy about breakfast on the beach is profoundly typical of his care for the bodily well-being of others during his ministry. Not only did he heal all manner of physical ailments, but he also had a keen awareness that people needed to eat.

❧ All four gospels depict Jesus wanting to feed the multitudes of people who came out to hear him teach: "Where are we to buy bread for these people to eat?" (John 6:5).

❧ The same care for crowds extended to individuals. After he attended the dying twelve-year-old daughter of a leader of the synagogue, "her spirit returned, and she stood up at once, and he directed them to give her something to eat" (Luke 8:55).

❧ Many were the joyful meals he shared with disciples as convivial settings for his teaching. Harsh was the criticism heaped upon his head for inviting socially marginalized people to the table: "The Son of Man came eating and drinking, and they say, 'Look, a glutton and a drunkard, a friend of tax collectors and sinners!'" (Matt 11:19).

❧ In a startling parable about the day of judgment, Jesus clarified the main criterion by which people will be judged: "for I was hungry and you gave me food. . . . I was hungry and you gave me no food" (Matt 25:35, 42).

❧ In teaching about divine care he used food for the birds as an illustration: "They neither sow nor reap nor gather into barns, and yet your heavenly father feeds them" (Matt 6:26).

❧ In a prayer still said around the world today, Jesus taught his disciple to pray to their *abba* for their daily bread in the same breath as for deliverance from evil (Matt 6:11–13).

❧ At his last meal he took a loaf of bread, blessed and broke it, and gave it to the disciples to eat with the words "Take; this is my body" (Mark 14:22); he also gave thanks over a cup of wine which all shared. This self-giving gesture of giving and consuming food became the core ritual celebration of the Christian community to this day.

❧ After his death and burial he walked unrecognized with two disciples on the road to Emmaus, until at supper "he was made known to them in the breaking of the bread" (Luke 24:35).

It is entirely in character, then, that a resurrection story depict Jesus being busy about feeding folks who are hungry after having worked long night hours on the lake. The physical action itself, "Jesus came and took the bread and gave it to them," rings with rich eucharistic overtones.

A Portal

Here a portal to a wider image of God begins to open. John's gospel has already identified Jesus as the Word of God made flesh, full of grace and truth. Whoever sees him sees the gracious One who sent him. Using the bodily sense of hearing rather than seeing, theologian Edward Schillebeeckx beautifully argues that Jesus not only told parables but is himself the parable that God is telling to the world. Whoever hears him hears what the Creator wishes to communicate. In a word, Christ is the sacrament of encounter with God.

"Come, have breakfast." Jesus's nurturing words and actions channel the living God's hospitality to the world, the driving divine desire that all should be fed.

Breakfast

Among all living creatures that sleep there is a well-nigh universal practice of eating upon awakening. Every morning when people and animals wake up to a new day, they need to take nourishment from the earth into their body. Doing so revives them from the unconsciousness of sleep and supplies fresh energy for the activities of the coming day. Of course, for people who work night shifts and for animals who are nocturnal hunters, this need to replenish comes at the other end of the sun's daily cycle. Either way, "breaking the fast" from food and drink that attends sleep is a fundamental biological need.

Human cultures the world over address this need in a dazzling variety of ways. Liquids are essential, so people drink water, coffee, tea and juices, and sip soups and broth. Grains of all kinds are processed and appear as breads, toast, pastries, pancakes, grits, rice cakes, noodles, congee, or hot and cold cereals made of oats, barley, and wheat. The protein of fish, meat, eggs, beans, and legumes makes an appearance, at times in soups and chilies. In some regions dairy products such as cheese, milk, yogurt, and butter enhance the menu. Fruits and jams add vitamins, as do vegetables like grilled tomatoes, mushrooms, corn, plantains, fried potatoes, sauteed bok choy, and members of the onion family. Flavors are enhanced by oils, sugar, honey, spices, and herbs. Then too, a slice of leftover pizza sometimes suffices.

The horror of hunger plagues millions of people today for whom there is nothing to eat for breakfast. Such a lack due to poverty emaciates human bodies and saps the spirit. In a searing way it stunts the physical and mental growth of children precisely by preventing them from ingesting the nourishment necessary for their young brains to develop and their muscles to grow strong. In 2021 UN statistics reported that "Globally, 149.2 million (or 22 percent) of children under the age of five years suffered from stunting," while an estimated 14 million children under the age of five worldwide suffer from acute malnutrition, also known as severe wasting.

The current global tide of hunger takes concrete form in headlines. After years of terrible drought that decimated their crops and livestock, villagers in the Horn of Africa, in Somalia, Ethiopia, South Sudan, and northern Kenya, leave their homes and trek for days across dust-blown wastelands to escape famine, ending up in refugee camps. In cities from Syria to Central America, families go to bed hungry. In Afghanistan, starving children stream into hospitals ill-equipped to treat them. On the planet as a whole, the scale of hunger is enormous. As of this writing, annual UN statistics continue to track upward as they record the millions of hungry people around the world. At the extreme end of the expanding spectrum of hunger, as many as fifty million people in forty-five countries are teetering on the brink of famine, according to the 2022 UN's World Food Program report.

While natural plagues of insects or crop disease are responsible in some instances, more often than not such conditions are created by complex unjust social, political, and economic structures and practices. Extreme weather due to human-caused global warming devastates once-fertile land. War disrupts the production and distribution of food. Global business practices allow some few people to accumulate excessive wealth at the expense of vast numbers of poor people and the environment. More precise analysis shows how deprivation is compounded by gender and race, with girl children and women in poverty as well as people of color more likely to skimp by on insufficient calories.

In a world where enough food is produced, the fact that children are wasting and people die of starvation is an outrage that cries to heaven. Amid such acute, unjust suffering, the divine summons to "Come, have breakfast" resounds with prophetic challenge. It cracks through the complacency of privileged people with insistence: stop global warming, make peace, change unjust business practices, feed the hungry, make it possible for every last person to start the day with nourishing food.

The Story's Reach

Human beings are embedded in a complex biosphere formed in part by other living creatures who also need nourishment. Plants, insects, animals—none would survive and reproduce without taking in material from the earth, directly or through other creatures. This very flow of physical substances through ecosystems and the bodies of every individual is what defines Earth as a living planet.

Given that animals inhabit such diverse habitats, salt and fresh waters, the skies, underground burrows and vastly different landscapes above ground, their breakfast menu is even more varied than the human one. Some eat vegetation, the grass, leaves, bark, fruit, flowers, seeds, and nectar of the plant kingdom. Others hunt for nourishment from fellow animals, the insects, worms, smaller birds, fish, rodents and mammals they evolved to prey upon. In this matter, death and life are tightly interwoven. The lifestream of one creature is given up as it flows into the new day of another. "They die into each other's life; they live from each other's death," the adage goes. The price paid for ongoing life in an evolutionary world, though exceedingly high, is natural. What is not natural in our day is the horror of animals dying of hunger and thirst, and even of whole species going extinct due to human destruction of their habitats.

Does this matter to God? It does if we understand that the risen Jesus's interest in feeding others reveals God's nurturing care that extends to the whole community of creation. Note the connection between Jesus's action on the beach, taking bread in his hands and giving it to the disciples, with the divine action depicted in Psalm 145. This psalm praises the Creator for being gracious and merciful, slow to anger and abounding in steadfast love, good to all and compassionate over all that has been made. Within this framework it continues: "The eyes of all look to you, and you give them their food in due season. You open your hand, and satisfy the desire of every living thing" (Ps 145:15–16).

What a wonderful poetic image this psalm offers: the eagle eyes of the raptor, the multifaceted eyes of the house fly, the reflective eyes of the cat, all animal eyes looking to God for food, and God open-handedly obliging. Other biblical texts paint the same picture. Amid lyrical descriptions of the bounty of the natural world, Psalm 104 describes how "the young lions roar for their prey, seeking their food from God" (v. 21). In a similar manner Psalm 147 praises God who prepares rain for the earth, makes grass grow on the hills, and "gives to the animals their food and to the young ravens when they cry" (vv. 8–9). Alerted to this idea of the Creator as feeder of lions and ravens, we might notice anew the concluding words of the creation story in Genesis 1:

> God said, "See, I have given you every plant yielding seed that is upon the face of all the earth and every tree with seed in its fruit; you shall have them for food. And to every beast of the earth and to every bird of the air and to everything that creeps on the earth, everything that has the breath of life, I have given every green plant for food." And it was so. (vv. 29–31).

Obviously, this is a vegetarian diet. According to the opening chapters of the Bible, eating meat made its appearance only after the catastrophic flood occasioned by great human wickedness. The literary genre of these texts prevents us from interpreting them literally. They are primeval stories of origin crafted with the intent to teach religious, not scientific, truths, truths such as God made everything that exists, and sinful actions can have ruinous consequences. In fact, lions were roaring for their prey (which was certainly not green plants) long before humans evolved with a capacity for sinning. The point to be noticed here is that precisely as origin stories these texts point explicitly to the Creator as the kind of God who takes a great interest in feeding people as well as "every living creature of all flesh that is on the earth" (Gen 9:16).

The Giver of life who creates and sustains all creatures also wills their good, that they should flourish. The risen Jesus's invitation to "Come, have breakfast" is not an isolated oddity but a vital expression of God's nurturing relationship with all creatures of the living world. Let this powerful three-word phrase reverberate beyond the scripture text. When we say the word "God," let us hear this invitation to breakfast. Let it impel us to act for just distribution of food in human communities and protection of nourishing habitats for animals. The living God, Creator of heaven and earth, passionately desires that all should be fed.

Come, have breakfast.
—John 21:12

Afterword

I started working on these meditations in the early part of my ninth decade on this planet. During the time of writing the crisis of global warming worsened, with all too real disastrous effects on human beings and other living creatures. Enormous efforts are being made to turn the ship around, but maybe not enough to avert coming disaster that I will not be here to see. We are on the brink, and the future can go either way. My hope has been to contribute to these saving efforts from the field of religion, as many colleagues are doing.

Having done scholarly work on ecological theology for over a quarter of a century, I thought perhaps a meditative approach would open a window for a wider group of readers. If people took time to ponder and even to pray with the meditations, then more human beings might come to realize that the natural world belongs at the core of loving care that comes with belief in God. This could unleash spiritual power in individuals and whole church communities with a positive, practical effect. Much more work in this area remains to be done. It is a blessing that younger theologians are taking up the challenge.

Whatever the particular subject, for me, teaching, writing, and public lecturing have always been an invitation to students, readers, and listeners to "Come and see," as Jesus invited some inquirers to do (John 1:39). Insight cannot be forced. As Vatican II's *Declaration on Religious Freedom* wisely recognized, "The truth cannot impose itself except by virtue of its own truth, as it makes its entrance into the mind at once quietly and with power." It seemed to me that the genre of meditation lent itself to the invitation to come and see, raise questions, make connections, think, explore, see for yourself how beautiful the faith tradition is, as a step toward encountering the vivifying holy mystery whom people call G-o-d. Then, grounded in this Ground of being, to go forth actively to love Earth and all its creatures, humans included.

In the interest of readability I did not stick with one translation of the Bible but searched for renderings that would fit a more colloquial style. While using mainly the New Revised Standard Version, I also drew from the website biblegateway.com which has over sixty translations of the Bible in English.

One recurring stumbling block was the address to God as a "lord," which appears frequently in scripture. As printed in English, the word is spelled in a unique way, with a large capital letter L and the letters ORD also capitalized but in a smaller font, thus LORD. By agreement among publishers, the word in this form represents the divine name revealed at the burning bush, YHWH. This is a mysterious name, often connected with the verb "to be" and translated "I am who I am," or "I will be with you." In the original Hebrew the name is not gendered. This allows for a great sense of the mystery of the living God, Creator and Savior of the world.

Clearly LORD is not an accurate translation of YHWH. Clearly, too, it is problematic. Rendering the divine name into English this way inevitably gives a masculine and patriarchal tilt to the holy mystery to whom it refers. At times I simply substituted God for Lord. At other times I tried to subvert the "lording it over" tone by adding an adjective such as good, gracious, bountiful, just, generous, trustworthy, or courteous. "O Lord our God" became "O sweet Lord our God." While not literally accurate, this is at least closer to the meaning of the original, especially when understood through the example of Jesus Christ, the Lord who washes feet. The problem of gender remains, however.

One of the delights in writing these meditations came from the way they continuously immersed me in the vital issue of how to speak about the mystery of God. This was the subject of my doctoral dissertation and first published article, and has been a passionate concern in all the decades since. It goes without saying that the great living God who creates and sustains the world and bears it toward the future cannot be fully captured in any one image, name, or concept. In fact, unfortunately, this usually does go without saying. The truth that the living God is beyond our understanding and that our words connect us but do not define God without remainder is seldom referred to in preaching or teaching. Yet this truth is basic. Our finite minds cannot comprehend the infinite. Our finite hearts cannot grasp love without limit. So we look toward God not as an object within the range of creatures but as the Ground of being, the Beyond in our midst, the all-encompassing, generative Creator Spirit with a heart for every creature.

Scripture is replete with reminders. Isaiah sounds a wake-up call: "To whom, then, will you liken God? Or what likeness compare with divine greatness?" (40:18). The prophet presses home the point: Have you not known? Have you not heard? God is the everlasting Creator of the ends of the earth! Look up at the stars, each one created by the Creator who calls every one of them by name. There is simply no comparing God with anything or anyone else. The prophet Hosea channeled God's own voice on the same point: "I am God and not man, the Holy One present among you" (11:9).

Centuries later the apostle Paul noticed an altar in Athens dedicated "To an unknown god," and proceeded to enlighten the citizens of that fair city. We know that God made the world and everything in it, giving life and breath to mortal humans and all living things, he preached. We also know that the Creator of heaven and earth is not far from any of us, for in this divine presence we live, move, and have our being. This precious knowledge leads us to realize that "we ought not to think that the deity is like gold or silver or stone, an image formed by the art and imagination of mortals" (Acts 17:29). No idol will suffice. This same Creator, so powerfully creative and so intimately near, raised a man from the dead. How beyond our art or imagination!

Granted, they laughed at him. But Paul's point is well taken.

It is salutary to pause and sit with the truth that the living God is infinite love beyond imagining. Whatever similarity we spy is forever encompassed by a greater dissimilarity. The living God is always ever greater.

Lest we despair, there is another way to come to know God besides thinking and speaking with words and images. It is the way of love. Augustine gave eloquent voice to this wisdom when he wrote, "If you comprehend, it is not God," meaning if you think you have fully understood God, you have deceived yourself. But if you wish to know something of God, he figured, then you should attend to your loving, for God is love. "In loving we already possess God as known better than we do the fellow human being whom we love. Much better, in fact, because God is nearer, more present, more certain."

Even with this, insists Aquinas, we do not grasp God's essential reality, which is beyond our capacity as creatures to comprehend. In the end we are united to God "as if to an unknown." Forgetting this, we reduce the infinite Creator and Savior of the world to our own dimensions and end up with a lesser god. Remembering this, we are liberated from confining ideas and images and led ever more profoundly into experiences of awe and adoration.

These meditations draw on the reality that there are many ways to speak of the living God. Each one is valuable, some more, some less, though not one of them delivers complete understanding. This in itself is a humbling kind of knowing. I have found it makes it easier to grasp myself as a human creature in the marvelous community of creation.

I offer warmest thanks to Robert Ellsberg and the team at Orbis Books who facilitated the journey of this book into print with gracious ease. My deep gratitude to the following colleagues who offered critical comments on drafts while these meditations were under way, or who tracked down references and helped with scripture translation: Charles Curran, Colleen Griffith, Mary Jane Haemig, Roger Haight, Nancy Hawkins, Mary Catherine Hilkert, Mary Maher, Maria Pascuzzi, Paul Schutz, Terrence Tilley, and Mark Travnik. It takes a village.

> *Teach us to discover the worth of each thing, to be filled with awe and contemplation, to recognize that we are profoundly united with every creature as we journey towards your infinite light.*
>
> —*Laudato Si'* 246

References

Introduction

Pope Francis, *Laudato Si': On Care for Our Common Home.* Vatican City, 2015. Quotes from this encyclical (a teaching letter) will appear in this book as *LS* followed by the paragraph number.

Stephen Jay Gould, "Unenchanted Evening," in his *Eight Little Piggies: Reflections in Natural History* (New York: Norton, 1993), 40.

Sea shells: Karl Rahner, "Priest and Poet," *Theological Investigations*, vol. 3 (Baltimore: Helicon Press, 1967), 296.

James Michener, *The Source* (New York: Random House, 1965), 120.

Creation: A Relationship

1. Your creatures

The singer and her song: Herbert McCabe, *God, Christ and Us*, ed. Brian Davies (New York: Continuum, 2003), 103.

2. Kin in the community of creation

Our blood is red: Arthur Peacocke, "Theology and Science Today," in *Cosmos as Creation*, ed. Ted Peters (Nashville: Abingdon, 1989), 32.

4. A suffering world

Charles Darwin, *On the Origin of Species by Means of Natural Selection* (New York: Barnes & Noble Classics, 2004; originally 1859), 384.

The cougar's fang: Holmes Rolston, *Science and Religion* (New York: Random House, 1987), 134.

Theodicy itself an evil: Terrence Tilley, *The Evils of Theodicy* (Eugene, OR: Wipf and Stock, 2000).

John Courtney Murray, *The Problem of God* (New Haven: Yale University Press, 1964), 6–11.

Denis Edwards, "Every Sparrow that Falls to the Ground," in his *The Natural World and God: Theological Explorations* (Adelaide, Australia: ATF Press, 2017), 89.

6. Creation's praise

The flea: Augustine, "Exposition of Psalm 148," *Expositions of the Psalms*, vol. 3, trans. Maria Boulding (Hyde Park, NY: New City Press, 2004), 485.

"Let your mind roam": Augustine, "Second Discourse on Psalm 26," *On the Psalms, Ancient Christian Writers*, vol. 29 (New York: Newman Press, 1960), 272.

7. Animals and the God of all flesh

Thomas Aquinas, *Summa Theologiae* I.75.5.

Ken Stone, *Reading the Hebrew Bible with Animal Studies* (Stanford, CA: Stanford University Press, 2018), 163.

The Vivifying Presence of God

8. Earth, a dwelling place of God

Julian of Norwich, *Showings*, trans. Edmund Colledge and James Walsh (New York: Paulist Press, 1978), 183.

Martin Luther, "That These Words of Christ, 'This is My Body,'

Still Stand Firm Against the Fanatics," *Luther's Works*, vol. 37 (Philadelphia: Fortress Press, 1955), 59–60.

9. Like water, like air

Augustine, *Confessions*, VII:7.

World-mothering air: Gerard Manley Hopkins, "The Blessed Virgin Compared to the Air We Breathe," *A Hopkins Reader* (Garden City, NY: Doubleday, 1966), 70–73.

Dante, *The Divine Comedy: Paradise*, canto 33, line 145.

Earth's the right place for love: Robert Frost, "Birches," *Selected Poems of Robert Frost* (New York: Holt, Rinehart and Winston, 1963), 77–79.

10. Like fire that ignites

Hildegard of Bingen: Mystical Writings, ed. Fiona Bowie and Oliver Davies (New York: Crossroad, 1990), 91.

Stephen Hawking, *A Brief History of Time* (New York: Bantam Books, 1988), 174.

Thomas Aquinas, *Summa Theologiae*, I.8.1.

11. The wisdom of the owl

Thomas Aquinas, *Summa Theologiae*, I.103.6.

Denis Edwards, *The God of Evolution* (New York: Paulist Press, 1999), 47.

12. The author of beauty

Ed Yong, *An Immense World: How Animal Senses Reveal the Hidden Realms Around Us* (New York: Random House, 2022), 5.

Creator with dazzling imagination: W. Norris Clarke, "Is a Natural Theology Still Possible Today?" in *Physics, Philosophy, and Theology*, ed. Robert Russell et al. (Vatican City: Vatican Observatory Press, 1995), 121.

World as primordial sacrament: Dorothy McDougall, *The Cosmos as Primary Sacrament* (New York: Peter Lang, 2003).

John Haught, *The Promise of Nature* (New York: Paulist, 1993), 76–78; also *Resting on the Future: Catholic Theology for an Unfinished Universe* (London: Bloomsbury, 2015).

Jesus and the Earth

13. Messianic peace

Richard Bauckham, *Living with Other Creatures: Green Exegesis and Theology* (Waco, TX: Baylor University Press, 2011), 110.

14. Salvation is on its way from God!

Edward Schillebeeckx, *Jesus: An Experiment in Christology* (New York: Seabury, 1979), 115.

Kin-dom of God: Ada María Isasi-Díaz, *Mujerista Theology: A Theology for the Twenty-First Century* (Maryknoll, NY: Orbis Books, 1996).

15. The gaze of Jesus

The list of animals and plants in Jesus's sayings was compiled by Richard Bauckham, *Living with Other Creatures*, chapter 3, "Reading the Synoptic Gospels Ecologically" (Waco, TX: Baylor University Press, 2011), 63–78.

16. Born of a woman: God with us, the kangaroos, the grasses, the soil

Martin Buber, "On Education," in his *Between Man and Man* (New York: Macmillan, 1966), 83.

Karl Rahner, "Christology within an Evolutionary View of the World," *Theological Investigations*, vol. 5 (New York: Seabury Press, 1975), 176.

Charles Darwin, *On the Origin of Species by Means of Natural Se-*

lection (New York: Barnes & Noble Classics, 2004; originally 1859), 434.

Niels Gregersen, *Incarnation: On the Scope and Depth of Christology* (Minneapolis: Fortress Press, 2015), p. 18.

Sallie McFague, *The Body of God: An Ecological Theology* (Minneapolis: Fortress Press, 1993), 161.

17. The cross and the tree of life

Jesus was not eaten by a lion: Michael Lee, "Historical Crucifixion: A Liberationist Response to Deep Incarnation," *Theological Studies* 81, no. 4 (2020): 895.

M. Shawn Copeland, "Wading through Many Sorrows: Toward a Theology of Suffering in Womanist Perspective," in *A Troubling in My Soul: Womanist Perspectives on Evil and Suffering*, ed. Emilie Townes (Maryknoll, NY: Orbis Books, 1993), 120.

James Cone, *The Cross and the Lynching Tree* (Maryknoll, NY: Orbis Books, 2011), 21–23.

Ignacio Ellacuría, "The Crucified People," in *Mysterium Liberationis: Fundamental Concepts of Liberation Theology* (Maryknoll, NY: Orbis Books, 1993), 580–603.

Niels Gregersen, "The Cross of Christ in an Evolutionary World," *Dialog* 40, no. 3 (2001): 205.

18. Deep resurrection: hope in God

Karl Rahner, "Easter: The Beginning of Glory," in *The Great Church Year*, ed. Albert Raffelt and Harvey Egan (New York: Crossroad, 2001), 191.

Ambrose of Milan, *Patrologia Latina* 16:1354.

Hans Küng, *Eternal Life? Life After Death as a Medical, Philosophical, and Theological Problem* (Garden City, NY: Doubleday & Co., 1985), 114.

homecoming: Küng, *Eternal Life?*, 113.

19. Salvation even for elephants?

Ken Stone, *Reading the Hebrew Bible with Animal Studies* (Stanford, CA: Stanford University Press, 2018), 142.

Edwin Teale, *The Wilderness World of John Muir* (New York: Houghton Mifflin, 2001), 317.

20. A world of grace

Karl Rahner, "Christology in the Setting of Modern Man's Understanding of Himself and His World," *Theological Investigations*, vol. 11 (New York: Seabury, 1974), 225.

Denise Levertov, "The Avowal," *The Stream and the Sapphire* (New York: New Directions, 1997), 6.

Kathryn Tanner, *Christ the Key* (New York: Cambridge University Press, 2010), 275.

Humankind and Otherkind

21. Dominion? Genesis 1 or Job

Bill McKibben, *The Comforting Whirlwind: God, Job, and the Scale of Creation* (Grand Rapids, MI: Eerdmans, 1994), 63.

22. Nature, a neighbor

Phyllis Trible, *God and the Rhetoric of Sexuality* (Philadelphia: Fortress Press, 1978), 75–82.

Robin Wall Kimmerer, *Braiding Sweetgrass: Indigenous Wisdom, Scientific Knowledge and the Teachings of Plants* (Minneapolis: Milkweed Editions, 2013), 10.

Brian Patrick, in Michael Dowd, *Earthspirit: A Handbook for Nurturing Ecological Spirituality* (Mystic, CT: Twenty-Third Pub., 1991), 40.

John Paul II, "Peace with God the Creator, Peace with All of Creation," Message for World Day of Peace, January 1, 1990, #16.

23. Pebble, peach, poodle, person

Thomas Aquinas, *Summa Theologiae* III.91.1 and 91.5.

24. Praying: we and us

Carl Sagan, *The Dragons of Eden* (New York: Random House, 1977), 11–18.

Henry Beston, *The Outermost House: A Year of Life on the Great Beach of Cape Cod* (New York: Henry Holt & Co., 1928), 25.

Phyllis Trible, *God and the Rhetoric of Sexuality* (Philadelphia: Fortress Press, 1978), 31–59.

God's Beloved Creation

25. Two Books

Augustine, "Sermon 68:6," *Sermons* III/3, trans. Edmund Hill (Brooklyn: New City Press, 1991), 225–26.

The July 11, 2022 televised unveiling of the first photo from the Webb telescope is available on YouTube.

Report on baleen whales: *National Wildlife* 60, no. 4 (June-July 2022): 10.

26. Biodiversity: dazzling, disappearing

Thomas Aquinas, *Summa Theologiae* I. 47.1.

Denis Edwards, *Ecology at the Heart of Faith* (Maryknoll, NY: Orbis Books, 2006), 78.

2019 report on extinction: United Nations, Intergovernmental Platform on Biodiversity and Ecosystem Services, "Global Assessment Report on Biodiversity and Ecosystem Services."

Jonathan Schell, *The Fate of the Earth* (New York: Avon Books, 1982), 117.

Suicide by proxy: UN General Secretary António Guterres, December 2022.

28. The rock of my heart

Martin Luther, "The Large Catechism," *The Book of Concord*, ed. Robert Kolb and Timothy Wengert (Minneapolis: Fortress Press, 2000), 386.

29. Under your wings

Aldo Leopold, *A Sand County Almanac* (New York: Oxford University Press, 1949), 32.

Gerard Manley Hopkins, "The Windhover," *A Hopkins Reader*, ed. John Pick (Garden City, NY: Doubleday & Co., 1966), 50.

Augustine, The Literal Meaning of Genesis Vol. 1, trans. John Hammond Taylor (New York: Newman Press, 1982), 41.

"As the wings of doves": Robert Murray, "Holy Spirit as Mother," in *Symbols of Church and Kingdom* (London: Cambridge University Press, 1975), 315.

"The world considers you": E. Pataq-Siman, *L'Expérience de l'Esprit d'après la tradition syrienne d'Antioche; Théologie historique* 15 (Paris: Beauchesne, 1971), 155.

The Prayers and Meditations of St. Anselm, trans. S. Benedicta Ward (New York: Penguin Books, 1973), 153–56.

30. Come, have breakfast

Edward Schillebeeckx, *Christ the Sacrament of Encounter with God* (New York: Sheed and Ward, 1963).

Afterword

Vatican II, *Dignitatis Humanae*, par. 1.

"If you comprehend": Augustine, *Sermo* 52, c.6, n. 16 (PL 38:360).

"In loving": Augustine, *De Trinitate* 8:8,12.

Thomas Aquinas, *Summa Theologiae* I.12.13.

Index of Biblical References

(following the order of books in the *New American Bible*)

Old Testament

New Testament